TWAYNE'S WORLD AUTHORS SERIES

A Survey of the World's Literature

AUSTRALIA

Joseph Jones, University of Texas, Austin

EDITOR

Randolph Stow

TWAS 472

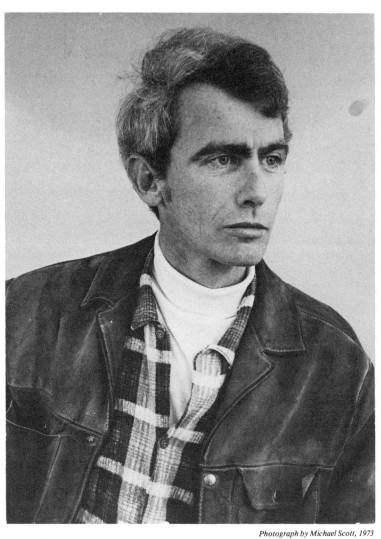

Photograph by Michael Scott, 1973

Randolph Stow

RANDOLPH STOW

By RAY WILLBANKS
Memphis State University

TWAYNE PUBLISHERS
A DIVISION OF G. K. HALL & CO., BOSTON

Library of Congress Cataloging in Publication Data

Willbanks, Ray.
    Randolph Stow.

    (Twayne's world authors series; TWAS 472: Australia)
    Bibliography: p. 151-55
    Includes index.
    1. Stow, Randolph, 1935-   — Criticism and interpretation.
PR9619.3.S84Z95   823   77-21611
ISBN 0-8057-6313-9

MANUFACTURED IN THE UNITED STATES OF AMERICA

Contents

About the Author

Ray Willbanks was educated at the University of Alabama, where he studied creative writing and at the University of Texas, where he received his doctorate in Commonwealth literature in 1972. It was while at the University of Texas that Mr. Willbanks began to read the work of Randolph Stow, an interest which led him to write a doctoral dissertation on the novels of Randolph Stow and later this TWAS book. Currently, he is an assistant professor of English at Memphis State University, where he teaches courses in American literature and creative writing.

Preface

Randolph Stow is a poet, a novelist, a librettist, a writer of short stories, and a critic. He is a man of significant talent. For this reason he merits study. He is also a major Australian writer, and for the student of contemporary literature, an acquaintance with Australian writing grows increasingly important.

This book is divided into eleven chapters. The first gives a brief biographical background of Randolph Stow and places him in the history of Australian literature. In Chapter 2, which begins the study of Stow's novels, and in succeeding chapters, my purpose is twofold. Recognizing that many readers are unfamiliar with Stow, or are unfamiliar with all the works, my first concern is to summarize the individual work. I begin the treatment of each novel with a recreation of Stow's story, sampling passages to give the reader as much of a sense of the novel as is useful. An analysis of the novel is presented either in conjunction with this or after the introduction is complete, depending on the demands of the specific novel. With each novel I deal with significant critical opinion, not only for the purpose of accepting or rejecting the critic's view, but also to indicate to some degree what the critics have found needful of discussion. Added to these points are my observations and judgments. I follow Stow's chronology, giving a chapter to each novel, indicating as I deal with each new novel its relation to the novel or novels that precede it.

In dealing with Stow's poetry I give a chapter to each volume, selecting as many representative poems as space allows, discussing Stow's themes, his technique, his successes, and his problems. Because there has been only a small amount of published criticism of Stow's poetry, and since of that amount little has been available to me, I do not refer to critical comments as I do with the novels. And since I am limited in space, I do not deal with the few poems that have been published since *A Counterfeit Silence* or that were not included in the three volumes. Following the poetry chapters is a brief chapter labeled "Other Works," dealing with Stow's children's book, two short stories, and two librettos.

The final chapter is an overview, divided into two sections: the novels, the poetry. There is a discussion of subjects, themes, and techniques. Following the poetry conclusion is a final statement concerning Stow's work.

RAY WILLBANKS

Memphis, Tennessee
February 1977

Acknowledgments

I wish to thank Professor Joseph Jones, retired, of the University of Texas, Austin, for introducing me to the work of Randolph Stow, for encouraging this study, and for editing the manuscript.

I wish also to thank Mr. Jock Curle of Macdonald and Jane's for his enthusiasm and for his considerable aid in securing certain publications of Randolph Stow.

Special thanks to Memphis State University for a Faculty Research Grant in the fall of 1976 which made certain aspects of researching this book possible.

I wish to thank the following publishers for their permission to quote from the works of Randolph Stow: Macdonald and Jane's: *A Haunted Land, Act One, The Bystander, To the Islands, Outrider, Tourmaline,* and *The Merry-Go-Round in the Sea;* Angus and Robertson: *A Counterfeit Silence.*

I am deeply grateful to Randolph Stow for an interview in January 1977, and for copies of ''Dokónikan'' and *Outrider.*

Chronology

1935   Julian Randolph Stow born in Geraldton, Western Australia, November 28; parents Cedric Ernest and Mary (Sewell) Stow.

1952   Attends Guildford Church of England Grammar School, near Perth.

1953–   At seventeen goes to the University of Western Australia;
1956   begins to write. *Act One, A Haunted Land,* and *The Bystander* written during these years.

1956   Graduates with B.A. degree from the University of Western Australia; *A Haunted Land* published in London.

1957   *Act One* and *The Bystander* published in London; *A Haunted Land* published in New York and translated into German. Receives The Gold Medal from The Australian Literature Society. Works among the aborigines for a few months on the Anglican Mission at Forrest River near Wyndham in northwest Australia; teaches English at the University of Adelaide.

1958   *To the Islands* published in London. Wins the Miles Franklin Award, Melbourne Book Fair award, and Gold Medal of the Australian Literature Society. Studies anthropology at University of Sydney.

1959   Moves to New Guinea, takes job as assistant to the government anthropologist. *A Haunted Land* translated into Dutch. *To the Islands* published in Boston.

1960   Returns to Australia from New Guinea; travels to England. Signs contract for *Outrider. To the Islands* translated into German.

1961   Does postgraduate work in English, University of Western Australia.

1962   *Outrider* published. Teaches in England at the University of Leeds. Writes *Tourmaline* while at Leeds. *To the Islands* published in Australia.

1963   *Tourmaline* published, London. Spends summer in Malta where he writes "Thailand Railway." Teaches at the University of Western Australia.

1964   Harkness Fellow of the Commonwealth Fund; travels in forty-six U.S. states. Writes *The Merry-Go-Round in the Sea* in New Mexico. Edits *Australian Poetry, 1964* (Angus-Robertson).

1965   *The Merry-Go-Round in the Sea* published, London; *Tourmaline* published in Australia.

1966   *The Merry-Go-Round in the Sea* published, New York. Receives Britannica-Australia Award. "Magic" published.

1967   *Midnite* published in Melbourne; Englewoods Cliffs, New Jersey; and London.

1968   *The Merry-Go-Round in the Sea* translated into Hebrew. "Dokónikan" published.

1969   *A Counterfeit Silence* published, Sydney. "Eight Songs for a Mad King," set to music by Peter Maxwell Davies, performed at Queen Elizabeth Hall, London.

1970   *Midnite* translated into Japanese, Dutch.

1971   *Midnite* translated into Danish. "Eight Songs For A Mad King" recorded, London.

1972   *Midnite* translated into German.

1974   Returns to Australia on a Commonwealth Literary Fund grant. "Miss Donnithorne's Maggott," music by Peter Maxwell Davies, performed at Adelaide Festival (Australia) and in London. *Randolph Stow Reads from His Own Work* recorded for the University of Queensland Press Poets on Record Series.

CHAPTER 1

Background

JULIAN Randolph Stow was born in 1935 in Geraldton, a small town some three hundred miles north of Perth on the west coast of Australia. Geraldton is bounded on one side by the sea and on others by farms stretching into the outback. The sense of sea, of sky, of space, of light and color are the impressions that play upon the people who live there, and that play with particular intensity on the creative sensibility. Geraldton and its surroundings form the setting for many of Stow's poems and for four of his five novels. For the reader unfamiliar with this part of the world, the Geraldton countryside rendered through Stow's work provides an exotic display of paddocks blooming yellow, fields of pink heather, strange trees: blackboys and blue jacaranda, skies filled with the crying of plovers and cockatoos and the screeching of parakeets.

Randolph Stow comes from "an old station-owning family of style, education, and eccentricity going back to the beginnings of Australian settlement in that [the Geraldton] area. Amongst his ancestors there are also South Australian pioneers, some of them formerly devout, as the Stow Memorial Church in Adelaide bears witness. A more bizarre ancestor is Pocahontas."[1] Stow's mother's family, which claim Thomas Jefferson as a relation, were pastoral pioneers in the Geraldton district. In addition to his mother and his father, who was a lawyer, Stow shared his childhood with a sister two years younger. He describes his childhood in numerous poems, but deals with it, with his family and relatives, extensively in his novel *The Merry-Go-Round in the Sea.*

Stow was educated in state schools in Geraldton. In his teens he left Geraldton during the school terms to board at Guildford Grammar School near Perth. He wrote quite a bit as an adolescent, but by his own description, most of what he wrote was in heavy imitation of the Romantic poets and Scottish balladists, with several verse plays in imitation of Christopher Fry.[2]

13

At seventeen Stow went to the University of Western Australia where he planned to study law, but he later changed to arts. Soon afterwards he began a serious attempt to write.

"I became a writer," he says, "for two reasons. One was that in the National Service I first collided with the facts of life in the atomic age. The other was the death of a friend. He was not a particularly close friend, but we were at school and college and Law School together, and to me his death, coming at that time in my life, was a pretty world-shaking experience. I felt it was terribly necessary for me to do something creatively and do it quickly. I expressed this at the time in a poem called 'Madame Yuan Disoriented' and that was really my first poem — the first, that is, that wasn't simply a literary exercise. Later that year I began *A Haunted Land*."[3]

A Haunted Land was published in 1956 when Stow was only twenty-one. *Act One,* a gathering of poems he had published previously and a number of new ones, was published in 1957. A second novel, *The Bystander,* was published the same year. In December of 1957, after spending time on an Anglican mission near Wyndham in Northwest Australia, Stow returned to Geraldton and began his third novel, *To the Islands,* published in 1958. Three novels and a book of poems — and by now Stow had arrived at the age of twenty-three. Like many writers, Stow was first discovered away from home. He was published in both London and New York before he was published in Australia.

At twenty-three, with the publication of *To the Islands,* Stow was a much discussed young man. In Australia the novel won the Miles Franklin Award and was also a Book Society Recommendation. Critics disagreed as to the worth of the novel; many were quite enthusiastic in their praise: Granville Hicks in *The Saturday Review of Literature* wrote, "Universal is a large word, but if it can ever be used it can be applied to *To the Islands*...."[4] Other critics were more reserved, taking an attitude of let's wait and see what he does next. Still others insisted on pointing out the similarity between this novel and Patrick White's *Voss,* which had been published the year before. These critics saw the works as a new phase in the growth of the novel as an art form in Australia. But whatever stand the critics took, they were paying attention to Randolph Stow. Articles began to appear in the major Australian journals, grouping the novels, discussing Stow's themes, his use of myth and poetry. Stow's reaction to all this attention was not predictable. In 1959 he decided to give up writing and he moved to New Guinea to take a job as an assistant to the government anthropologist. The work was primarily linguistic and it was work which interested him, for he had majored in French at the University of West Australia and had also acquired a fluency in Spanish. Bad health forced Stow to give up the New Guinea post after eleven months, but the experience in the Trobriand Islands gave him material for two stories, "Magic" and "Dokónikan," and several poems. He returned to Australia for awhile, and in 1960 went to England where he signed a contract with his London publisher for a new collection of poems. The result was *Outrider,* a book illustrated by the Australian painter Sidney Nolan. The book was delayed for several reasons and was not published until 1962.

Stow returned to Australia and for some time did postgraduate work in English at the University of Western Australia. In 1962 he again went to England, this time as an assistant lecturer in English at the University of Leeds, where he taught a course in Conrad.

In 1963 Stow published *Tourmaline,* his fourth novel. Although Stow repeated the approach in *Tourmaline* that he had used in *To the Islands,* working with his story along the lines of the mythic and the symbolic, *Tourmaline* marks a decided maturity in Stow's ability to integrate the elements of his fiction.

Only two years passed between the publication of *Tourmaline* and Stow's last novel to date, *The Merry-Go-Round in the Sea,* but with *The Merry-Go-Round in the Sea* came a complete departure from the form of the previous two novels. Gone are the allegorical implications, the symbolic approach. Instead Stow writes a poetically realistic story of his childhood, drawing his characters not from ideas, but from his family and his boyhood friends. Stow decided to write the novel while traveling in the United States, describing its conception thus:

While driving around Florida, I began to think of writing this book; mapped it out one night in a Louisiana motel, continued writing it in my head all over Texas and New Mexico, and finally, when the snow first arrived, settled down in a shack on an apple-and-beef ranch near the Colorado border and wrote it in seven weeks. I tried to re-create something of the feeling I had about Australia when I was six years old or so, and it seemd that Japan could take Australia with one armoured division and would do it.[5]

Since 1965 Stow's creative output has slackened. In 1966 he published a children's book, *Midnite,* and in 1969 a book of selected poems, *A Counterfeit Silence.* Although the collection contains ten previously unpublished poems, written during the years 1954-1966, the book is primarily made from poems published in *Act One* and *Outrider.* Also in 1969 his *Eight Songs for a Mad King,* a poetic sequence set to music by Peter Maxwell Davies was given its first performance. In 1974, Stow again collaborated with Davies, writing the poems to Davies' music for "Miss Donnithorne's Maggot," performed first at the Adelaide Festival, and later in the spring in London. Both musical compositions have been recorded. Also in 1974, Stow was recorded reading a number of his poems for the Poets on Record Series for the University of Queensland. Since 1974 Stow has taught a university course in Denmark, and now makes his home near London in Essex where he continues to write.

Before getting into the study of Stow's work, it might be of value to make a few observations concerning Australian literature in general and Stow's relation to it. Literary historians usually divide Australian literature into three periods: (1) the colonial period, stretching from the beginnings of settlement to around 1880, with the literature produced primarily by Scottish, Irish, and English immigrants. Writing both poetry and prose according to English models, the Australians were often concerned in fiction with the adventures of immigrants and the horrors of the penal system. Fiction was for the most part realistic, descriptive, episodic, while poetry was usually descriptive, often sentimental. (2) The nationalist period, usually dated from the year the Australian periodical the *Bulletin* was founded, 1880, to the end of the First World War. Writers came to see themselves as Australians rather than colonials. Again the writing, particularly the fiction, was primarily realistic, humanistic, and often intensely patriotic in its insistence on Australian ideals. (3) The modern period, 1918 to the present. From World War I to the fifties, literature became less concerned with an insistence on Australian national themes, though the element is still present. Some writers, Henry Handel Richardson, for example, turned to individual themes. Of consistent interest to the writers were social problems, particularly the problems of the working class. Throughout this period, as in previous ones, there was a continuing interest in Australian history and pioneering adventures, and although there was some modern experimentation in poetry beginning in the 1930s, poetry continued in a conventional manner, both descriptively realistic and descriptively romantic, depending on the poet and his subject. Similarly, although there were exceptions, fiction prior to the 1950s was still mainly realistic.[6]

T. Inglis Moore, in his *Social Patterns in Australian Literature,* identifies a number of concerns that occur repeatedly in Australian literature. Among the concerns are those he describes as follows: (1) "the spell of the bush," the writer's fascination with rural Australia, the outback and the desert; (2) "the clash of cultures," the basic conflict of white against abo, the clashes among the various immigrant groups against each other and against the dominant group; (3) "the creed of mateship," man's dependence on his fellowman, a dependence often made necessary by the vastness of the land and its demands; (4) "the Great Australian Dream," emphasis on the wealth of the land and the possibilities for a new life and a new man; (5) "radical democracy," a strong, sometimes radical insistence on the rights of the individual man; (6) "humanism," an emphasis on this world rather than the possible one to come, humanistic, rather than religious, concerns. Among the attributes of traditional Australian literature that Moore finds typical are those of "irony," "sombreness," and "realism."[7] Stow's poetry makes use of a number of these traditional subjects, and the poetry as a whole is nonexperimental.

Beginning in the 1950s certain writers — notably Patrick White in *The Tree of Man* (1955) and *Voss* (1957), and Randolph Stow in *A Haunted Land* (1956) and *To the Islands* (1958) — published novels that were a distinct departure from the traditional Australian novel grounded in realism. Instead of the observation of the outward man, these novelists turned inward. From the realistic approach, White and Stow moved to the romantic, the poetic; both writers began to explore their themes in terms of symbol and myth. During the late 1950s and on into the 1970s, other novelists have moved in a similar direction.

Randolph Stow's fiction, then, is basically a departure from the long line of Australian novels that come before it. Though he does touch upon some of the traditional concerns in his fiction — for example, the use of the bush or desert setting in *To the Islands* and

Tourmaline; the clash of cultures with the use of a Balt immigrant as a central character in *The Bystander;* and the presentation of the abo-white problem in the mission setting of *To the Islands* — the inclusion of these traditional elements is only part of the story he is telling, never the basis of the story as it has been in earlier novels.

There is irony in Stow's work, particularly in *The Bystander* and in certain poems, but for the most part his use of irony is incidental, and in the novels never a dominant note. Of sombreness, which Moore tells us is characteristically brought about by the uncertainties as man faces the elements and the magnitude of the country, there is quite a lot in Stow, particularly in the poetry. The "cry of the crow" often breaks the silence and opens up the loneliness of space in his novels and in his poems as it does in traditional Australian literature, but if there are drab, mocking crows, there are also bright chattering parakeets and cockatoos.

If Stow is traditional, he is in the tradition of Western literature in general rather than in a particular Australian tradition. It is interesting to note that in his listing of writers who have influenced him — Elizabethan and Jacobean dramatists, Eliot, Pound, Rimbaud, St. John Perse, Garcia Lorca, Whitman, and (as a poet) D.H. Lawrence — only two Australians are included: Judith Wright, who, he says, "has had a profound effect on my way of looking at the Australian landscape"; and Patrick White, whom he had not read until he had already published two novels.[8]

In order to examine Stow's works individually and at length, let us consider the first of the novels, *A Haunted Land.*

CHAPTER 2

A Haunted Land

RANDOLPH Stow published his first novel, *A Haunted Land,*
in 1956, when he was twenty-one. It is not a major work, and
of Stow's five novels it is the slightest, but at the same time it has
merit. Stow tells a good story; he creates a fictional world as self-
contained and as compelling in its own way as a Faulkner or a
Brontë world; and he tells his story in a highly imagistic prose that
provides in itself a reward for the reading. In a study of Stow's
work, *A Haunted Land* is important for another reason; it provides
the earliest illustration of thematic concerns that preoccupy Stow
throughout his fiction.

I *Plot*

In order to provide a background for a critical consideration of
the novel, a re-creation of Stow's story is useful.

The setting for *A Haunted Land* is the country near Geraldton
and Dainton, two small coastal towns in western Australia. Most of
the action occurs on the stations (farms in this case) Malin, Koolabye, Strathmore, estates whose distant boundaries touch each other
in interlocking patterns suggestive of the relationships of their
owners. The period is the time of the Boer War.

The central character is Andrew Maguire, Irish owner of Malin.
The name *Malin,* suggesting sickness, evil, is a symbolic extension
of the personality of Maguire, and is further suggestive of the interior life of the station; and it is the illumination of this interior life
that concerns Stow in the novel.

In the first chapter Maguire's wife dies and three of the five children are sent away from Malin to schools in Melbourne. The story
proper begins with the second chapter. Ten years have passed and
the children, now young adults, have returned to Malin. The action

19

of the novel is compressed into a period of one year, from early summer to the week before Christmas.

Adelaide the eldest girl looks from the buggy as the three children approach their home:

> The same Malin. Shabbier now, its white walls less white and its green paint less green. The lawns looked unkempt and the flower beds had broken bounds and spread into the drive. But the same Malin, surrounded with the privacy of trees, the same smoke rising blue from one of the chimneys at the back.[1]

The personalities of the five children are individualized as the narration progresses, but none of the children matters quite so much as Andrew Maguire, their father, who is the main force, the wicked child, and the malicious patriarch of Malin. A man of overbearing pride and selfishness, Maguire willfully destroys his children through an obsession to re-create in them the characteristics of his dead wife. Maguire's physical appearance, his youthfulness, is often distorted by his raging anger. What Stow accomplishes through the description of the ever young Maguire is the suggestion that his youth is maintained through a kind of demonic spirit that nourishes rather than dissipates. The question of Maguire's sanity is ambiguous throughout most of the novel, and the reader's attitude toward Maguire wavers in much the same way that his children's do.

Completing the household of Malin are Mr. and Mrs. Cross, caretaker and housekeeper, and their idiot son Tommy, a hairy creature who walks on all fours and lives in a wire cage. There are also the black workers, an uncanny whippet named Lash, and a cat given to periodic spells of insanity.

The story is tragic. Maguire lives for three things: the love he maintains for his dead wife, the devotion he requires of his children, and his contempt for those neighbors and relatives who are not Maguires. Throughout the novel his love for his wife and his contempt are unchanging; the story lies in his destruction of his children, as one by one he destroys their love affairs, their self-respect, or their love for each other.

The irony in the novel comes from the fact that Maguire has no concern for the welfare or happiness of his children; he is interested only in what the children bring to him and in the way in which their personalities reflect his own. Nick, the second son, has been kept from a music career, as Patrick, the youngest, is kept from law, being told by his father, "We Maguires can't live in a crowd and crowds can't live with us" (55). On Patrick's first night at home he is called into the "book room" to join Nick and their elder brother Martin as a drinking "accompaniment" to their father. That Nick at eighteen does not drink is a sign of weakness to Maguire and before the night is over the three sons and the father form a drunken quartet. This becomes the nightly habit, the purpose of which seems to be to lighten Maguire's chronic melancholy. Thus, Stow paints a picture of a drunken and demonic father, and three unhappy and subservient sons.

Anne, the younger daughter, bears both a physical and a psychological resemblance to her dead mother, and thus she is Maguire's favorite. Anne revels in her own privateness, her strangeness. She is pretty and consumptive, as was her mother, and feels herself isolated by what she believes to be her impending death. Fond of poetry, she frequently quotes from *Measure for Measure.* "Be absolute for death," lines her mother had read aloud years before.

Adelaide, the elder daughter, like Martin, the eldest son, is the practical, dependable, workhorse of the family. But unlike the other members of the family, she has a certain clear-sightedness. She is aware of the crosscurrents and the underlying instability of Malin. From the first night at home she thinks, "Something is wrong here; one can feel a whole series of quarrels..." (45). And yet on another level she reflects: "An early summer morning at Malin, and nothing is changed...nothing is changed. The same sunbeam ferries in dustmotes from the balcony; in the kitchen a pile of saucepans is knocked over. A gate slams in the yard, a dog barks. Cross is bringing the milk" (36).

Such is the surface life of Malin, but as the months of summer pass, the disintegration of the family begins. First, there are little things, things brought about by Maguire's manipulation of his children. Maguire feels that Patrick, the youngest, is weak, and as an initial test of his courage, Maguire sends the unknowing son in the company of Adelaide to view the Cross's monstrous offspring, Tommy. Maguire watches the whole affair, "grinning his devil-child's grin" (55).

The verandah on one side of the cottage was fenced off with strong wire mesh and shaded with the red tecoma which brought the ants to trouble Mrs. Cross. And in that enclosure Adelaide saw something move.

It was man and animal, a creature lying on its side on the floor and scratching itself with long fingernails. Its hair was long, but combed, its faced covered with a thick black down; its hands and arms were those of an ape, thick and strong, covered with tough black hair. Lying on the floor, it scratched itself — dressed in a clean shirt and bright blue overalls.

. . .

The creature on the floor stirred like a wakened cat and jumped up on all fours, stared at them with the narrow eyes of a wolf.

Patrick saw it, and said: "Oh Jesus Christ in Heaven!" (73)

The two flee from Tommy Cross and run into the still grinning Maguire. Adelaide has dropped her handkerchief and Maguire sends Patrick back for it. Afraid, Patrick refuses to go. Maguire accuses him: "The blind eyes seemed somewhere deep down to burn, the taut lips showed pain. I should never have sent you away,' he said softly. 'I should never have let you leave Malin to become what you have become: a degenerate, a coward...'" (56). Patrick, white with shame, returns to Tommy Cross. Maguire joins him.

Presently Maguire stepped forward to the cage, and stung Tommy Cross on the cheek with a flick of his finger. Tommy Cross fawned on the wire and howled like a dog.

. . .

For a long time Patrick neither moved nor looked at him. Then he too stepped forward to where Tommy Cross rubbed himself against the wire. And he seized Tommy Cross's forelock and pulled it, standing his ground, though Tommy Cross hurled himself on the wire and spat at him, though he bit at the wire till the corners of his mouth were bloody. (56)

This scene is important for several reasons: it introduces Tommy Cross, who is necessary in the working out of the plot in the novel; it illustrates the basic cruelty of Maguire; and it gives specific insight into the conditioning of the boy Patrick, a conditioning that leads him later to murder on behalf of his sister Anne.

It is to Anne that the first major event in the novel happens. Hot from riding one summer afternoon, Anne strips and swims in an isolated pool. After her swim she suns herself, lying naked by the pool. Sexually stirred by her day-dreaming, Anne does not flee when she realizes that she is being watched by the black youth Charlie. Moments pass, Anne wonders — "'He has seen something, he has seen something in my face,' she thought." She remembers a line from a novel: "... to have lived a long time ago and loved a bushranger or a convict ... an outcast ... someone lonely...." And she thinks before he takes her sexually: "Natives aren't people" (73). Later, in fear and self-loathing, she tells Patrick, who remembering his father's disgust at his apparent cowardice, shoots the youth.

Anne withdraws into herself, and this begins the rapid crumbling of the family structure. Nicholas, feeling that his father despises him, has the courage to flee Malin for Perth and points beyond, but true to his father's prediction, he cannot exist beyond Malin and he falls into drunkenness and dissipation. Martin, also feeling the frustration of his father's dissatisfaction, tries to find a place for himself by leaving Malin to marry. Seeing Martin's leaving as an ungrateful attack on him, Maguire suggests to the impressionable Martin that he has inherited the family insanity that will manifest itself as he grows older. Martin marries in the face of the warning, but he believes his father and the marriage is a miserable one.

Patrick, despite his murder of Charlie, is the most likeable and certainly the most vital of the Maguires. In what is one of the finest sections of the novel, Patrick falls in love with, pursues, and has an affair with Jane Leighton, a young widow from nearby Koolabye. When Maguire learns of his son's love, he plays upon Patrick's innocence by offering to convince Jane's mother of the rightness of the affair, knowing that the mother will remove her daughter from the country when she learns Jane is involved with a Maguire. Although the plan is never carried out, Patrick's revelation of it to Jane causes the two to argue over the motivation of Maguire and his desired rupture occurs.

The climax of the novel comes one stormy December night, even as the now pregnant Jane is coming from Koolabye to Malin to bring about a reconciliation. The hatred and violence Maguire has encouraged is brought to fruition on this night. In the midst of the rising storm, the whippet begins to cry. Patrick goes out to investigate. What follows is seen through Adelaide's eyes.

She did not remember how she came to the back verandah, but once she was there every detail was clear. She saw the lamp set down carefully on the boards, showing that Patrick had not been taken unawares but had seen what was there and had gone to meet it. She saw the two figures struggling, rolling, wrestling in the grass and heard the animal snarling of Tommy Cross.

Anne's voice behind her was saying: "Patsy! Patsy!" and did not seem to raise itself above a whisper.

And she saw Maguire come out and stand on the edge of the lawn, poising the rifle, waiting his chance. (211)

In the confusion Maguire shoots his son, then kills Tommy Cross.

Two sons gone from Malin. One dead. Anne distracted, having lost in Patrick her one support. Adelaid left to endure. But Maguire is not yet defeated, nor is his malice quelled. He forces the Crosses to remain quiet about the manner of Patrick's death, and prevents them from giving Tommy a Christian burial. His final bit of evil, or insanity, whichever it is, comes at the private burial of Tommy. Mr. Cross is reading the service, Adelaide and Mrs. Cross are attending, when suddenly Maguire, partly drunk and grieving over Patrick, comes riding out of the trees and into the cemetery.

Maguire carried a long stake that he had cut while he was waiting. Anne trailed behind him, looking lost and not interested in what he was doing.

Maguire walked his horse to the edge of the grave, so that Adelaide had to move aside for him. He looked around him mockingly, at the dark earth that covered Tommy Cross, at Adelaide, at Cross. He did not look mockingly at Mrs. Cross.

He said pleasantly: "I didn't shoot him with a silver bullet, so ... shall we make sure that the werewolf is properly dead?"

He leaned over and drove the stake deep into the earth over the coffin.

Mrs. Cross gave a thin scream. Adelaide reached out and seized her wrist, but she did it automatically and without looking away from Maguire. Then his eyes came round to her again and they stood and stared at each other across the stake that was still quivering in the grave.

At last she said huskily: "Are you mad? Or are you a child?" (223-24)

From this point, the novel moves rapidly to its conclusion. Jane leaves with her mother to have her baby in Ireland. Anne, unable to stay at Malin, leaves also for Ireland, where presumably she will die from tuberculosis. Adelaide is left alone with Maguire. She, for the first time, faces up to her father's madness and what her life is likely to be, left alone with him in the lonely Malin. Yet it is only when Maguire begins to express self-doubt to her, the possibility he has been wrong, that Adelaide sees a mission for herself; and her conception of this mission shows her own capitulation to her father. She cannot allow him to doubt the rightness of his actions. For her own security she must help him to keep his ego intact, for it is by his ego, his concepts, that she has structured her own being.

A warm breeze came in through the open window, bringing the familiar sick and poisonous perfume. And she, sobbing, fell on her knees beside him as he sat in the window seat and took his arms and shook him, in anger and despair, crying:

"It's not your fault! It's *not your fault!*" (250)

So much for the plot of *A Haunted Land.* From such a summary, the novel is likely to seem contrived, its content slight, its achievement hardly more than that of entertainment. But such is often the case when a novel is reduced to its story line. Consider, for example, what one is left with when he reduces to its plot *Wuthering Heights,* a novel with which *A Haunted Land* has been compared. What matters in both novels is the way in which the story is handled, the language, the structuring of the action, the total effect of the interplay of character, setting, and action. Sometimes Stow is successful; sometimes he is not, as an analysis of the novel will show.

II A Haunted Land *as Romance*

First, it seems necessary to try to come to terms with the type of novel Stow is writing in *A Haunted Land.* Critics have viewed the novel in different, yet vaguely similar ways. P.H. Newby writes that *A Haunted Land* "...bore many of the marks of the Poet's novel."[2] He remarks that the story was decided by the people in it, and adds, "There was no intervention from history — no gold strike, no drought, no war — to reduce the scale on which personality had been conceived. Happenings come about because these people are these people and for no other reason."[3]

Vincent Buckley writes, "We have arrived perhaps in the era of the lyrical-realist novella."[4] David Martin says, "This is a poet's novel, both positively and negatively. Positively because it is rich in feeling and intuition, and negatively because no novel can be outstanding in which the lyrical element, however well transmuted into psychology, dominates characterization.''[5] Geoffrey Dutton, after briefly comparing *A Haunted Land* and *Wuthering Heights,* concludes:

In many respects, however the Brontë comparison is accurate and useful, for it reminds us of the lineage of the kind of novel Mr. Stow is writing. The main tradition of the English novel is not of this kind — the tradition that is, of Fielding, Jane Austen, George Eliot and James. [In] . . . some of Dickens and in several American novels we can trace another, the tradition of the novel as dramatic poetry — and it is to this that Mr. Stow's book belongs.[6]

What have we come up with? The "poet's novel"; the "lyrical-realist novella"; the novel in "the tradition of the novel as dramatic poetry"; the novel that has "aspired toward the condition of poetry." A term that for some reason is absent from these descriptive definitions is the old-fashioned, but it seems to me quite serviceable, term, *romance.* If a label is helpful in understanding a work of fiction, and sometimes it is, then perhaps under the umbrella of the label *romance* a good number of the aspects of *A Haunted Land* that critics have found objectionable can be acceptably accounted for.

But first, let me clarify my use of the term *romance.* As applied to *A Haunted Land,* I am thinking more in terms of the contemplation of Hawthorne than of the action of Scott, more in terms of the mythic quality of Emily Brontë than of the character studies of Henry James. In *The Scarlet Letter,* for example, Hawthorne presents his characters as types, Chillingsworth, the man of cold intellect; Dimmesdale, the man of weakness and emotion. In this respect the flesh and blood nature of the characters, their individuality, is made subordinate to the representative role Hawthorne intends them to play. The ideas that are illustrated through the conflict of the characters in their Puritan background are of greater importance to Hawthorne.

Setting is quite important in *The Scarlet Letter;* the story in part *is* the New England village. Emily Brontë makes her setting, the natural aspects of it, carry even more importance than does Hawthorne. To a great extent Heathcliff and Katherine are extensions of the winds and storms and spaces of the moors of Wuthering Heights. The novel as a whole fits well the definition Hawthorne worked out for himself in the Customs House section of *The Scarlet Letter,* describing a romance as "that neutral territory, somewhere between the real world and fairy-land, where the Actual and the Imaginary may meet, and each imbue itself with the nature of the other."[7] With this definition in mind, and with Hawthorne and Brontë as examples, let us look at *A Haunted Land.*

In Chapter Two Nick, who is an amateur artist as well as a musician, opens a folder of drawings and shows them to his inquisitive sister Adelaide. There are six sketches, each representing a different member of the family:

She laughed at the sketch on the top of the pile, an extraordinarily mocking and affectionate representation of Martin as a draughthorse. Everything about it, the heavy hooves, the bony face, was perfect. Martin's beard had become the long hairs that sprout from a draughthorse's chin. The whole drawing expressed solidity and clumsy goodwill.

"That's wonderful," she said, and laid it aside.

Patrick was, in Nick's eyes, a very nervous and belligerent bullock. He glared at the beholder from a lean, square-jawed face and lashed an impatient tail.

. . .

He had drawn Anne as a fox, and she noticed again the too sharp satire that she was sure he had not intended. The fox's face wore a perfect parody of Anne's bitter smile. . . . (133)

Nick represents himself as a lamb, Adelaide as a cat, and finally they come to the sketch of Maguire:

They looked down at the drawing. It showed Maguire as the Serpent, the most vicious and brilliant caricature that Adelaide had ever seen. His long, hipless body had become a snake's, without actually ceasing to be his own human frame. It was clothed in breeches and ended in boots and was twined ridiculously and horribly around a tree. From beneath the lowest branch Maguire's face leered at them, his head thrown back and his chin thrust towards them. The mouth was a snake's mouth, and yet it had Maguire's thin smile. The eyes too, cynical and strange, were their father's. (134)

Leonie Kramer, who has perhaps written more extensively about Stow than any other critic, looks at this scene and comments, "Stow here makes explicit what has been clear from the beginning:

in *A Haunted Land* he is an allegorist, translating into human shapes theories about human types."[8] Such a comment might also be made about Hawthorne and about the characters in a romance in general. Yet for some reason Kramer finds this approach objectionable. She continues: "*A Haunted Land* demonstrates in a crude and particularly accessible form what happens when a novelist adopts an anti-realistic position in relation to his characters. Stow does not start with people, but with ideas about people. He does not examine relationships; he invents them."[9]

Kramer's last two sentences seem to further classify Stow as a romancer. And, at the same time, Stow's starting "not with people, but with ideas about people" does not necessarily indicate a fault. Kramer speaks of Nicholas's caricatures, and concludes that although the behavior of the Maguires is consistent with the caricatures, the behavior

> ...has no springs; and when Stow occasionally tries to look directly into their minds, it is of his bewilderment rather than their inner life that he gives a glimpse.
> Thus, though they appear to live, the Maguires are apart from life. It is something of a shock to hear them speak of Melbourne, for they live in a world of nightmares and fairy tales. Patrick Maguire surely makes the understatement of the novel when he says of Malin, "Everything about it is sort of strange."[10]

What Kramer is complaining about is a further example of her failure to recognize what Stow is doing in the novel. A "world of nightmares and fairy tales," a world where "everything about it is sort of strange," is precisely the kind of romance world that Hawthorne describes as "that neutral territory, somewhere between the real world and fairy-land, where the Actual and the Imaginary meet...." While Kramer obviously has a point in wanting all the life she can get from characters, I find myself reaching again to Henry James and his insistence on granting the writer his *donée*. Kramer is asking that Stow make Maguire and his children in-depth studies of individual personalities. Perhaps the more "life" a character has, even in a romance, the greater the possibility for reader enjoyment, but granting Stow his objectives, how much can we fault him and how important is character delineation?

In fact, Kramer seems to be contradicting her own opening state-

ment on the novels of Stow in general. I quote this in full, for it
seems to be an excellent statement of what Stow is all about.

It is important to recognize that Stow espouses the cause of the anti-
realistic novel, not because he has tried realism and found it unworkable,
but because it provides him with the scope he imagines himself to need. In
choosing to write an anti-realistic novel, he is of course in one sense immediately relieved of the burden of imposing some order and consistency
upon human behaviour. Character becomes a function of plot, and more
particularly of symbolism; it need not, indeed cannot, be explored *per se.*
We do not go to an anti-realistic novel to gain insight into motives, open
and concealed, of human beings, or better to understand their loves and
hates, their successes and triumphs. We go to it for an experience, or series
of experiences of a quite different kind.[11]

If Kramer is correct, and I think she is, then the importance of
Stow as a writer, particularly in the first novel, is not marred by his
use of characters who are types, certainly when the use is a delib-
erate one and is consistent with the kind of novel he is writing.

A further aspect of romance that is found in *A Haunted Land* is
that the characters often take on a mythic quality, a dimension
somewhat larger than life. Again, the characters in *The Scarlet
Letter* and *Wuthering Heights* serve as examples. In *A Haunted
Land,* Maguire, depending on which character is describing him,
assumes both satanic and deific proportions. Serpent images
abound from the relatives and neighbors, and from the drawings of
Nicholas; but more typical of Maguire's children's view of him is
the one found in a passage in which the analytical Adelaide con-
siders her father: "If she had been able to prove to herself that he
was not sane she knew that she could have felt only pity for him,
never love. But she did love him, and she could not help herself.
She loved him as Christians loved God, with adoration and terror,
loving and fearing" (130).

It is not until the final chapter that the reader is given any insight
into the character of Beth, the wife whom Maguire has obsessively
mourned. She seems a fit mate for a fiendish husband, and she is
pictured wandering about the countryside, hunting, and killing
with cruelty:

"By the time I came up to her the dog had cornered the kangaroo and they
were fighting and she was all white and shaking, gripping the whip tightly

and calling out to the dog. She had a beautiful voice, but I was afraid of her for a moment. When the dog had killed the kangaroo she picked him up and kissed him and carried him back to the sulky in her arms." (243)

Like Maguire Beth enjoys physical violence, and when as a child Nick refuses to hit his brother Martin, she hits him with her whip and says, "You're not one of us; you cringe" (243).

And Anne; clever, with red hair and quick eyes; the fox. In a Lawrencelike scene Stow extends the humanness of Anne into her animal duplicate. Riding over a rock ridge one day Anne comes upon a fox cub. She takes it up, and clutching it, meets the eyes of its mother:

And then her instinct told her that she was being watched, and she looked up and met the angry, desperate eyes that were fixed on hers, and saw the vixen standing stiff-legged and bristling and the fine teeth showing under the snarling lip. Neither of them moved. They seemed frozen by one another's gaze, the fox and the girl who looked like a fox. . . . (182)

In what seems to be an effort to add to the larger than life dimension of his characters, Stow often resorts to quotations from English literature. Anne sometimes quotes long passages from Chaucer and frequently from Shakespeare. She is especially fond of the line, "Be absolute for death. . . ." While in this first novel the quotations are only mildly bothersome, seeming a bit awkward but neither really adding to nor detracting from the flow of the story, Stow is less successful with this device in later novels, particularly in *To the Islands*. What is first seen in *A Haunted Land* as an attempt to solidify or enlarge upon character develops in the later novel as a substitute for characterization, and the protagonist who moves through a wild and desolate countryside quoting English literature is simply unconvincing.

Further to Kramer's criticisms of Stow's characterization and my own view of the novel as romance, there are some other critical observations that need to be dealt with, particularly the charge that the events in the novel reduce its status to that of melodrama. Certainly there is always the possibility for — even likelihood of — melodrama in a romance. Consider the scaffold scenes in *The Scarlet Letter* or the beyond the grave communication between Katherine and Heathcliff in *Wuthering Heights*. In *A Haunted*

Land there is certainly enough sensationalism for melodrama: a bizarre dog, a crazy cat, a rape, a murder, sons who flee home, drunkenness, insane rages, a monster who breaks out of his cage, a father who kills his son — all in the space of some two hundred and fifty pages. There is no denying that the novel is in a sense melodramatic, and Stow is himself aware of this. Early in the novel he has Anne remark: "Life holds the mirror up to melodrama" (108). And so it does. One man's melodrama is another man's reality. The question that is of concern to the critic is not whether melodrama is present in the novel, but the degree to which it is present and the manner in which it is handled. One might well count the violent actions and the bodies in *Hamlet,* certainly in *The Duchess of Malfi,* and find all the ingredients for melodrama. It is not without good reason that numerous critics have pointed to the similarity between Stow's subject matter and his structure in this novel and that of Shakespeare and several Jacobean dramatists, particularly Middleton and Marston.[12] What saves *A Haunted Land* from a dismissal as insignificant melodrama is a blending together of the same qualities that save Shakespeare and the Jacobeans. There is enough attention to motivation, even though Stow's characters are based on types; and the manner of presentation, the language, the poetry, the structuring of the action, is of such quality as to make the violence and the sensational events acceptable.

III   *Style and Structure*

Although the critics differ in their appraisal of *A Haunted Land* as a whole, they all agree that the writing itself — the language, the images, the flow of words — is excellent. Critics refer to Stow as a "prose poet" or a "romantic poet in prose." Whatever the term, the prose is outstanding. Leonie Kramer writes: "One is conscious not of 'fine writing,' but of being conveyed directly by language into a place and into a mood. So lucid and self-effacing is his prose and so sensitive his selection of detail, that one is put immediately in contact with sights, sounds, and moods."[13]

Like Hemingway, Stow has the ability to turn any place into *the* place, to evoke the particulars of the setting. Consider his rendering of the West Australian countryside and Malin. In the Prologue of the novel, Jessie Cameron Maguire, Martin's wife, is returning to

Malin fifty years after the story proper. The following is her observation of the countryside:

> The road rose to the hills, the flat-topped hills with their great outcrops of grey rock. The sandplain became moorland covered with low-growing scrub out of which the blackboy thrust a forest of black spears. To the left the hills dropped down to an old river bed. From this height one could see back to the coast, to the sea like a flat stone shining under a sky as hard as metal.
> "This has not changed," said Jessie softly.
>   . . .
> There was the paddock where the cemetery was, beside a shady oak, and there the avenue of gums. They were like some strange exotic fruit trees, heavy with great white flowers, but as the car drew closer the flowers rose and flew away and the sky seemed filled with a storm of torn paper, and the scream of five hundred white cockatoos fell scolding on the dry air. (10)

And in Chapter One, on the day of the death of Beth Maguire, we come to a typical interior scene. Stow leads into it by calling the reader's attention to a sky full of birds. Notice how the color is carried from the birds to the room.

> A flock of green parrots screamed over the house crying "Twenty-eight! Twenty-eight!" As they passed, Adelaide started from her lethargy and sat up, folding her hands tidily in her lap.
> The room was green with the lilac tree outside and the half-drawn curtains. As if whelmed with the sea, the white walls, the stiff chairs, the old upright piano with its candlesticks and silk front, were all awash with green. Even the red-brown heads of her brother and sister, sprawled on the green carpet, were tinged with it. We are mer-children thought Adelaide. She felt that if she dared to undo her soft black pigtail it would float upwards like tendrils of seaweed above her thin face. She was nine years old. (13)

In the following passage as in the previous one, color is used repeatedly. The use of color is important to Stow, and over and over he lights his scenes with it, so much so that despite the death and violence and melancholy in the novel, the overall impression is one of light, of brightness and of color.

> Heath grew up in the hill, pink and matted, and the smell of it was hot

and rough in the strong sunlight. Above the heath little low bushes grew
out of the gravel, some bright with yellow flowers, others (the poison
bush) the colour of rust. (49)

In the brush the dwarf wattles were covered with great balls of yellow
down and coming to the hill she could smell the scent of the heath floating
down to her. As she struggled through the rough stems she broke off a
branch of it and the tiny pink flowers were thick on it like foam or rime.
Everywhere about her as she scrambled up the slope scrubby insignificant
bushes were breaking out in colour. The poison bush burned with hard
orange flowers and another anonymous shrub was covered with what
looked like buttercups. (180-81)

Sound is also important in Stow's description. As in Webster or
Shakespeare, Stow's skies are often filled with crying birds. Sometimes the birds and their cries are merely a part of the background,
as are the birds in the two passages previously quoted, but often
they are used to reflect the dominant mood in a particular scene or
to break the mood:

It was one of those warm, still Sunday afternoons that are like no other
afternoon in the week. In the paddocks the sharp tongues of mudlarks
scratched the air with cheerful quarreling, and even the cries of the distant
crows and the screech of a flight of green parrots had a sleep sound. Somewhere where he could not see, a plover was mourning — tew tew TEW te-
e-e-e-ew; weeping itself into drowsiness. (170)

But everywhere else was dryness and desolation, and the whole world
seemed stilled by the heat. Only when a flock of pink and grey galahs flew
over, screaming, was the silence temporarily broken. (50)

Aside from the beauty of Stow's descriptive passages, they
almost always serve to advance the plot of the novel. In particular,
he uses the changing seasons and changes in weather as structural
devices, paralleling the coming of storms and their breaking fury,
the droughts and ending of droughts, the coming of spring and the
coming of winter, paralleling these changes in the natural world
with the psychological instability, the periods of calm and crisis in
the Maguire family. Because in the working through the calendar
year the seasonal changes are normal, are expected, and in the
writing are prepared for, they serve the function of making the
family eruptions and violence seem less out of harmony with the

natural world that encompasses Malin. In the fineness of Stow's writing, the careful patterning of plot with environmental change helps to make the action credible and to reduce the sense of excessiveness that turns drama into melodrama. Such a patterning device is a very romantic one, and Stow's use of it suggests a further parallel between his methods and those of Shakespeare and the Jacobeans, as well as another parallel between *A Haunted Land* and *Wuthering Heights.*

Geoffrey Dutton, writing of Stow's use of nature as a structural device, is reminded of Hardy, but he is quick to point out that Stow does not share Hardy's sense of fatalism or determinism. The forces of nature often correspond to and in some cases help provoke the forces in man, but man is in no way determined by nature, either in the physical sense or in the sense of philosophical naturalism.[14]

Another structural method Stow follows in the novel is based on the entrances and exits of characters. Beth dies, three children leave; ten years pass and the children return; Nicholas leaves home; Martin leaves home and marries; after the death of Patrick, his lover Jane Leighton leaves for Ireland; and after all the exits, there remains only a self-doubting Maguire and the faithful, resigned Adelaide.

The only major criticism of Stow's structure of the action in the novel comes from his use of the monster Tommy Cross as a kind of *deus ex machina.* Stow, in an interview with John Heatherington, has pointed out that Tommy Cross is the only character in the novel based on a real person.[15] Be that as it may, the demands of art require that such a monster be made believable. G. K. W. Johnston sees Tommy Cross only in terms of a symbolic device and faults Stow for making him engage neither the reader's sympathy nor his horror. For this reason he finds the monster an unrealized element in the novel.[16] I disagree. He seems real enough; certainly Stow presents Patrick's and Anne's horror of him convincingly, and the reader can share their horror as well as he can share anything else that happens in the novel. I agree, rather, with Geoffrey Dutton, who sees the monster as "a touchstone for the Maguire pride of being unafraid";[17] it is for this reason that Maguire allows the Crosses to keep him alive. Dutton continues that he "...is not an excrescence; he is accepted as part of life at Malin, for these horrors do hide in the country. He is also symbolically integral to much of

Stow's thinking.''[18] Tommy Cross is convincingly described; his hatred of Maguire and Patrick is fully explained and his outbreak prepared for; I can find no reason to fault Stow for his use of him, particularly considering the novel in terms of the type of book Stow is writing.

Finally, we come to the question of meaning in the novel. The meaning is somewhat ambiguous, but this is not in itself a flaw. The work is about will and pride and selfishness, and it is also about love and the deviousness of love. Through Andrew Maguire one can see the corruptive nature of love, and through his children's regard for him one can also see the binding and the weakness that love creates in the lover. But Stow is not writing a psychological novel, and since his characters are more in the nature of types than they are studies of individuals, the subtleties of the love relationship are not worked out, although the basic problems are indicated. Love, pride, fear, manipulation, and the result of these things; it is here that the meaning of *A Haunted Land* lies. And while, in general, *A Haunted Land* is quite a respectable novel, one's final reaction to it as art is probably dependent on his taste for romance.

CHAPTER 3

The Bystander

STOW's second novel, *The Bystander,* has received the least critical attention of any of his five novels. To some extent this is
understandable, for the novel is the least experimental of the
group, and for this reason it has not stimulated the critical interest
of the others. It is not that the novel has been overlooked; it is
rather that in any general criticism of Stow's work, critics seem
more eager to pass over *The Bystander* as Stow's most conventional novel for the more controversial *To the Islands* and *Tourmaline.* In a sense this is a mistake, for *The Bystander* has fewer flaws
than the other novels. It contains some of Stow's best writing. It
continues a theme begun in *A Haunted Land;* and it prefigures
motifs that interest Stow in his later novels. Furthermore, in *The
Bystander* Stow creates one of his most sympathetic characters, the
half-wit Keithy. And finally, *The Bystander* is suitable for those
critics who would prefer that Stow do one thing at a time, i.e.,
either write an allegory or a realistic novel. *The Bystander* is the
closest that Stow has come to a novel of straightforward realism.

I *Plot*

Since the plot of *The Bystander* is uncomplicated, I shall include
some analysis in conjunction with the plot summary, thus departing
from the organizational method in Chapter One.

Waking out of the brief sleep into which she had fallen, she lay and
listened to the wheels of the train under her until they seemed to be questioning her — name, age, place of birth; weight, height, colour of hair —
and she lay analyzing her life into words that could be written along dotted
lines. Remembering places, a town in Latvia, a camp in Germany, a ship;
and then a migrant camp here in Western Australia, tin huts and gum

trees; a shop in a country town with a window full of aluminum saucepans and dead blowflies; a farm in the south where she had worked as cook. One place she would not remember, a house in Latvia that had been called, ten or eleven years ago, before the war, home.[1]

Diana Ravirs, a Balt migrant, is traveling to Lingarin, a station in the Geraldton area of Western Australia, where she will work as a housekeeper.

A fair pale girl stepped down on the platform, and he knew immediately that it was she. He watched her as she came slowly across towards him, looking round to see if someone had come to meet her. She was certainly goodlooking; handsome, cold and lonely in her cheap faded dress, holding the cardboard suitcase a little behind her, as if she were ashamed of it. Her hair was the colour of a paddock full of new stubble.
...Her eyes were astonishingly blue. Gold hair, blue eyes; if her face were not quite so strong she would make a heroine for a fairy tale. (11)

Bright and cold, cold as ice, frozen. As with Andrew Maguire in *A Haunted Land,* Diana's physical appearance is an outward display of her inward nature. Other images from this initial description, the cheap faded dress and the cardboard suitcase, are repeated elsewhere in the novel, and are to her a reminder on a very simple level of what the war, a concentration camp, migration, and life in general have taken from her. She is humiliated by the cheapness of her things, and it is in the beginning this need to acquire things that disguises from her her deeper needs. She resembles Abbie in O'Neill's *Desire Under the Elms* who above all else wants a "home." A hillbilly song becomes a refrain throughout the novel, and the last lines, "I don't want something for nothing, I just want something forever," make the simplest statement of the theme of the novel.

Frank Farnham, who along with his wife Kate is Diana's employer, meets her at the station and drives her to Lingarin, his farm. Though a great deal of the action occurs at Lingarin, Stow again uses the same area that he used in *A Haunted Land,* for at various times we are at Koolabye and Strathmore, stations in the first novel, and several scenes are set in the now dilapidated Malin.

Diana has been employed so that the Farnhams can return to England for a year, a dream that has held Mrs. Farnham's imagination for a long time. What they have not told Diana is that she will have in her care their retarded son Keithy, who, injured at birth, has not progressed mentally beyond the age of a child, though physically he is a young man. Stow introduces Keithy:

A green parrot flew into a fig tree and rested there, tearing at the fruit. He stirred in the hay and watched it. It was fat and brilliant. When shot it would fall to the ground with a plump thud. But he did not want to kill it. He sat up and threw a stone, and the parrot flew away, skimming low over the haystack, squawking as it went. He laughed and lay back in the sweet drowsy smell of the hay.

A joey, a small kangaroo, came round the corner and stopped, forepaws dangling watching him. He called to it: "Here, boy. Joey, here." and it hopped towards him. He caught it in his arms and held it. "Joey, Joey boy, you love me? You love me, boy?"

The white cockatoo sat on the verandah rail and screamed: "Keithy! Keithy!" It bounced up and down, screeching: "Dance, cocky, dance," jiggling the length of the rail and calling to the visitor. (13–14)

This first view of Keithy illustrates Stow's handling of his characterization, for the boy is made real through the things he loves. He is an innocent, and is, as Geoffrey Dutton describes him, ". . . a genuine child of nature, as all of his pets demonstrate, a blessed idiot in the old sense of *seely, saelig*."[2]

Significantly, Keithy is first physically described through the eyes of Diana, who discovers before she is told, that Keithy is not "normal."

He was of average height, broadly-built, and, in his way, good-looking; brown-haired, grey-eyed. . . . But there was a remoteness in his face that was strange. He stood quite still and silent in the doorway, three dead rabbits hanging from one hand, a rifle from the other, and looked at her with a curious considering expression in his eyes and his head tilted to one side.

. . .

Oh dear God, she thought, it is a fool. (23–24)

Humiliated by what she has perceived as a social slight and now having discovered that Keithy is to be her charge, Diana threatens to leave Lingarin. The last of the novel's three major characters, Patrick Leighton, a neighbor, a friend of the Farnhams, and Keithy's idol, is asked to deal with Diana, to talk to her about Keithy and to persuade her to stay. By reminding Diana that she has nothing and that the home will be hers for the year the Farn-hams are gone, Patrick is successful.

The reader will perhaps recognize the name Patrick Leighton as a combination of the names of the characters Patrick Maguire and Jane Leighton from *A Haunted Land.* Though not a sequel to *A Haunted Land, The Bystander* is a continuation of that story. Patrick Leighton is the bastard son of the lovers Patrick and Jane, born during his mother's exile in Ireland. In this novel, Patrick, already in his midforties, is a lonely, lame, bitter man. He is the heir to Koolabye and Malin, and like his mannish cousin Nakala, who lives alone at Strathmore, Patrick is an isolated figure, caring only for his land, for the past which he feels has cheated him, and for Keithy, whom he loves both as a son and as one more vulnerable and more sinned against than he.

The plot of the novel is formed by the conflicts in the relationships of Diana, Keithy, and Patrick. Each is in his own way a bystander, a misfit, a type that will occur again in Stow's subsequent novels. Kate Farnham, Keithy's mother, describes them: "She stood on the verandah and watched them go down the path to the utility, and she found herself thinking involuntarily: How pitiful. A lame man, a displaced person, and my poor simple boy. I don't suppose three such lost lonely people ever set out together with ideas of enjoying themselves" (126).

The father-son, pupil-teacher relationship between Keithy and Patrick has existed long before the story begins, and Stow needs only a couple of dramatized scenes to illustrate this relationship. On the other hand, he is most painstaking in slowly developing the subtle relationship between Diana and Keithy. In the beginning Keithy reacts to Diana as he reacts to his animals and to the natural beauty of the Australian countryside. She is a lovely and intriguing object. The first morning after her arrival at Lingarin, Diana goes for a prebreakfast walk, and Keithy, himself just getting up, sees her. He imitates the cry of a plover, then stamps his boots to attract her attention.

He was struck with admiration, studying her with his slow thinking eyes. "Your hair's lovely."
"Do you think?"
"It's like hay. No, better than hay."
"Thank you."

"Aren't you going to get dressed?"

"Yes," she said, climbing up the bank of red earth from the creek-bed and trying to hold her dressing-gown closed as she did so. She was embarrassed and angry to have him there watching her.

"Your slipper's got a hole in it. Why don't you get it mended?"

"I like to have a hole in my slipper."

"Do you?" he said naively. "I don't."

"In Germany everyone has a hole in her slipper. And in her clothes. It is the custom."

"Why?"

She shrugged. "Who can know? The English and the Russians and the Americans and the French thought it is a good custom for the Germans to have. And the Germans thought it is a good custom for the Latvians to have."

"What are Latvians?"

"I am a Latvian. I come from a country that you call Latvia."

"Are Latvians cruel to people? Germans are, I've seen it in the pictures."

"No," she said. "Latvians are for other people to be cruel to."

He considered it, and decided: "Well, no one will be cruel to you here." (41)

This rather long quotation ilustrates several things. One, Keithy's innocence. He sees and appreciates with the unconditioned vision of a child. Like a child, he questions, and it is on a later question and answer that the climax of the novel depends. Stow's overview of his characters and their situation is more ironical in this novel than in the first, and it is Keithy's statement in this scene, "Well, no one will be cruel to you here," that illustrates for Diana the central irony of the novel.

The quotation is also an initial indication of Diana's nature. She begins with Keithy in the same distant "cold" manner that experience has taught her to use with all people, but as the conversation continues, and it goes on for several pages, Diana begins to thaw toward Keithy:

...she let herself observe him closely, noting the way his straight hair hung over his forehead and the pleasant serious lines of his face, thinking that he was quite good-looking and that it was a pity that he was a fool. He was not shy or shifty as many simpletons are, and his abrupt way of speaking made him sound quite intelligent and adult. (43)

Diana lets herself be led by Keithy about the farm as he shows
her his blind dog, his ugly cat, his cockatoo, his pet snake. As often
happens in the novel, and in the tradition of Cooper and others
who have used a half-wit to speak the truth that the "competent"
character often misses, Keithy brings Diana into self-recognition.

> "You know why I hate snakes? It's because they don't love anybody."
> She swung round and looked at him, but there was nothing but simplic-
> ity and the pleasure of discovery in his face; he had not been thinking of
> her, had probably not even been seeing her as he spoke. But the remark
> hurt her like a jibe, and she was suddenly where she had always been,
> outside and alone. (46)

Paralleling Diana's developing affection for Keithy is the growing security she feels at Lingarin as she looks forward to the time
when the Farnhams will leave for England. She thinks, "'The
house will be my own.' Every time she thought of that, it gave her a
feeling of excitement. 'Something at last will belong to me, even if
it is not forever'" (76–77).

The inevitable turning point in the relationship of Keithy and
Diana comes one day when Keithy has taken her for a drive to see
the view from the top of a cliff beyond Malin. They must cross a
river that is flooding over the ford. Against Diana's protests,
Keithy, who is determined to cross the river, takes her in his arms to
carry her. Keithy stops in midstream, kisses Diana, and confesses
his love.

> She came back to him out of the dream and found him standing in mid-
> stream, staring at her as if he were lost; and then, as she looked round, he
> tried to kiss her, and she was afraid. It was not the kiss that terrified her,
> but his face. He said flatly: "I love you," and his face was intense and pur-
> poseful as any man's. She had treated him as a small boy, and suddenly,
> terribly, found that Keithy Farnham was not a child at all. (65)

Diana struggles free of Keithy and runs back to the truck, leaving
Keithy bewildered and angry. He is hurt, for he doesn't understand
what he has done and why Diana has run away. Stow's registering
of Keithy's confusion is one of the finest things in the novel. It
illustrates Stow's technique of filtering emotion through the landscape in such a way that both character and scene are one.

Near sunset, and a plover cried over the far paddocks, the green bowl of the hills. Through a rift in the clouds long rays leaned on the land, and the shadows of hills stealing away from that light were blue like clouds across the bright grass.

The light caught flakes of mica in the rock, where Keithy had kicked his heels against it as he sat there. Leaning forward with his arms on his knees he saw the bright fragments and scraped at them with his boot.

Things not understood can be haunting. He could not remember anything before that had so troubled him. Most things in life were easily acceptable; you did not question the form of clouds on the horizon or the composition of a flower. You did not wonder why you loved a dog, and killed rabbits. Those were normal things. Your parents knew what they were doing, you did not trouble yourself to find out why. Everything could be accepted but this girl who ran away and cried.

The plover wavered sadly closer, and he thought of his love, kicking moodily at the rock. He could not understand his love. There were other things he loved — his animals, his parents, Patrick — but that was a feeling that was somehow different. (76–77)

With Keithy's initiation, one made even more painful because of his inability to understand what has happened to him, his relationship with Diana is suddenly further complicated by the budding courtship between her and Patrick Leighton. With Diana's song "I don't want something for nothing, I just want something forever" playing in his thoughts, Keithy senses a double loss; he will lose Diana to Patrick, and Patrick will reject him for Diana.

The courtship is a brief one. Patrick wants a son and responds to Diana. Diana wants a home and sees Patrick as a man who can give her one; and in his thin physique, his loneliness, his tenderness towards Keithy, Diana finds him attractive enough to accept his proposal.

Against Keithy's protests, the marriage between Diana and Patrick occurs, but from the beginning it is an unhappy one. The honeymoon turns into a thing of bitterness. Diana is frigid, a condition she tries to explain in terms of what has happened to her in the concentration camp. Patrick is both hurt that she doesn't want sex with him and furious that she has married him knowing her own feelings. He sees himself cheated of the son he has wanted and accuses Diana of having married him only for material possessions. Much of the final third of the novel is given over to the bitter quarrels between Diana and Patrick. Keithy has been moved to Koolabye to live with Patrick and Diana while his parents are in England, and often finding himself in the midst of Patrick's rages against Diana, Keithy, siding with Diana, soon incurs Patrick's anger. As a final result, he runs away from Koolabye to live alone at Lingarin. Patrick, unable to persuade the miserable Keithy to return, sends his hired man Fred to cook for him.

Diana, too, after months of trying to live with Patrick, tries to run away; but Patrick, who both loves and hates her, brings her back, and withholding money and transportation from her, keeps her as a prisoner. Diana's only real happiness during these months, as it has been from the beginning, is Keithy, who provides her with a gentleness and peace.

Spring is for a time an interlude, and Stow again uses descriptive passages to parallel the beauty of nature and the beauty of Keithy. But as spring turns into summer, Keithy's simple world, already shattered, now disintegrates. Stow has introduced Keithy in the beginning of the novel in terms of his animals, as his nature is shown through his gentleness and love for them; and as Stow moves toward the climax of the novel, it is the death of two of Keithy's animals that precipitates the crisis and brings Stow to the end of his story. First, Fred, grudgingly living with Keithy at Lingarin, stumbles upon Keithy's pet snake in a shed, and frightened of it, he kills it. Keithy is enraged, for he can't or won't understand that it is an accident. Patrick further alienates Keithy by taking Fred's part.

The second accident is Keithy's fault and Stow describes it with a clarity and economy that is characteristic of his best writing.

Under Keithy's utility lay the old dog, comatose, drugged with age and heat. Flies swarmed over him and he did not flinch. His ears hung limp and turned as if he were dead.

Then Keithy came out of the house, and he was looking happy, because Fred had lent him ten shillings and he was going to Koolabye to give it to Diana. He came silently across the dead grass and got into the utility where there was no door. He started it and it jumped forward quickly, because it was in gear, and there was a bump. He stamped on the brake.

Then the old dog began screaming and screaming, and Keithy jumped out, saw him dragging himself away and screaming like a person who is in agony. Then the cockatoo began screaming on the verandah and the kangaroo came hopping around the corner to see what was happening there.

Keithy stood by the utility feeling sick, not believing that it had happened. But the screaming went on until the whole world seemed filled with it, and he was deafened and maddened by it until he could listen no longer.

He turned and ran away, and ran to the haystack and lay down and hid his face. (223)

Against all Keithy's protests, Patrick does what he must and kills the suffering dog. Miserably, Keithy takes the gun and forces Patrick to leave Lingarin.

Diana, understanding the depth and meaning of Keithy's loss, comes to comfort him, and in her own self-pity and bitterness towards Patrick, she begins to talk to Keithy about him:

"He wanted his pleasure, and he wanted a son for his land and his family, and would never listen to me or understand me or care. He would not stop a minute to know what I was thinking. Everything was him and I was nothing. In the books the men say they will go through fire and water, through fire and water they say; but he will not go through one hour waiting for me to learn what it is to love free. And so I tried to run away. But he has taken my money and he will keep me forever for his pride and to hurt me with his angry tongue."

He said softly: "Through fire? Did you say through fire?"

"Men you love," she said with a tremulous laugh, "say they will go through fire for the person they love. But Patrick would only go through fire for himself and his land."

"That's a—an ordeal," he said. (228)

In Chapter Four Keithy's mother has used the word *ordeal* in conversation with Diana, and at Keithy's insistence, she explains the word. Keithy has remembered the explanation and in the final chapter of the novel, he accidentally knocks over a lantern while in the woods setting traps. He is some distance from the woods, driving toward Koolabye when he looks back and sees the blaze and panics. As this is occurring, Diana is telling Patrick that she will leave him to return to Lingarin and care for Keithy until his parents return. A telephone call informs them of the fire and they hurry to Lingarin.

Diana and Patrick are separated in the business of fire-fighting and Keithy comes to her and we have the final scene of the novel.

When she turned, Keithy was behind her, his face absorbed and strange in the strange light. She said, "I thought you had gone, Keithy."

"I wanted to see you."

"Me? Why?"

"To show you this—all my trees burning—and I don't care."

"What do you mean—?"

"I love you more than my farm—not like Patrick."

"Oh, Keithy."

He came closer to her. "Do you love me?"

"Of course, Keithy."

"More than Patrick?"

"More—much more."

"You said that before, and you married him."

"I am honest, Keithy."

Then he looked at her, with the deepening strangeness in his face, and asked: "Would you have an ordeal for that?"

And as it had been that day at Malin when he had carried her across the ford, suddenly he had picked her up in his arms, and he was watching her. And for a moment she looked into his mind.

The faraway men beating at the fire could not hear her. She screamed and screamed again, and the sound went up to the sky, muffled, unreal. And he looked at her, half accusingly, she said softly: "I'd go through fire for you."

And she found herself lying on the ground....

He shouted over her: "I'd go through fire for you!" And he began to run into the trees, the powdery ash rising from his thick boots, thrusting against the heat with all the strength of his stifled terror, and his ignorance, and his love.

The lights of Nakala's truck, turning past the house fell on the white cockatoo, so that it wakened and flapped its wings and screamed: "Keithy! Keithy!" (237–38)

The conclusion is ambiguous and open-ended. The question of Keithy's death is left to the reader's speculation, as is the possibility of a reconciliation between Diana and Patrick, either with or without Keithy.

II *Characterization*

In terms of characterization, Stow moves from the flat figures, or types, in *A Haunted Land* to more fully realized individuals in *The Bystander*. He is not altogether successful, but his limitations, specifically with Diana and Patrick, are less significant than his achievements. The best thing in the novel, as I hope my selection of examples has made obvious, is his rendering of Keithy.

As in *A Haunted Land,* we find Stow drawing from the Jacobean dramatists; he begins *The Bystander* with a quotation from Middleton's *The Witch:* "Though the Fates have endued me with a pretty kind of lightness, that I can laugh at the world in a corner on't . . . yet let the world know, there is some difference betwixt my jovial condition and the lunary state of madness; I am not quite out of my wits" (Preface). The last line, "I am not quite out of my wits," suggests the latitude that Stow gives himself in his conception of Keithy. Although Keithy, unlike Middleton's character, is not aware of his condition, he is not a static character; he can learn and to some degree understand what he learns, and because of these abilities, he can change. The problem Stow faces in working with a character such as Keithy is that having once decided what Keithy's mental level will be, he must keep the character's abilities consistent. It is a difficult problem, but Stow handles it well. He places Keithy's mental age somewhere around twelve, and though Keithy is retarded, Stow places him at the outward range of retardation. Within his limitations he is intelligent and therefore capable of insights. To further keep Keithy's character consistent, Stow controls those scenes that are presented through Keithy's point of view. He tries to work on a middle ground, keeping the diction simple, comparable to a child's verbal ability, and yet consistent with the objective voice of the narrator. As an example, consider the scene in which Keithy is being teased by a visiting child. He is accused of having a girl friend — Diana. He is challenged, "Is she really your girl friend, Keithy?"

> He considered it, leaning on his spade. If there was a girl who went walking with you and rode on the tractor with you, and let you hold her to keep her warm, and carry her over rivers, and leaned her head on you and said, "I care for you, Keithy" — if there was such a girl, then she must be your girl friend. But if she also ran away from you and looked scared and cried when you touched her, was she your girl friend then? And he said, "I don't know." (93-94)

The narrator's voice and Keithy's voice come close to merging into one in this passage, and the record of Keithy's reasoning process further extends his characterization as he is shown to be thoughtful, patient, struggling for insight.

Although Stow in dealing with Keithy never slips far beyond the possibilities of Keithy's verbal level, in some scenes in which the narrator is both observing Keithy and observing through him, there is a bit of awkwardness, as the voice is obtrusively that of the narrator. Consider one of Keithy's rare trips into town. Two neighbor boys take him along and leave him to amuse himself as they play pool.

They took him to the billiard saloon and placed him down on a bench while they began a game. He sat and stared around him, momentarily interested by the lights over the green tables and the movement of the coloured balls, but after five minutes this palled. Painstakingly he read the notices, fly-specked and ancient, that hung around the walls. Some, rather brusquely, said: KEEP YOUR CIGARETTES OFF THE TABLES; others, more prim, PLEASE DO NOT USE BAD LANGUAGE. As his boredom increased, he considered using some bad language, and seeing what would happen, but refrained out of consideration for the Robsons. (110)

Words such as *momentarily, brusquely, prim, refrained* belong to the narrator rather than to Keithy, and as a result of this slightly elevated word choice, the reader is made aware that he is viewing the scene as the narrator views it and not solely as Keithy views it. Flaws like this, if one chooses to consider them as such, are infrequent, and for the most part the movement into Keithy's point of view is consistent and successful.

Keithy is further characterized and his changes registered by the opinion the other characters have of him, particularly that expressed by Diana and Patrick. In discussing Keithy's love for Diana, Patrick tells her: "But can't you see, if he grows up as much as that, if he starts wanting the same things that normal people want — well, what'll happen to him? What chance has he got to be happy that way? He'll just be a deformity, and he'll know it before long'" (145).

Their attitude toward Keithy also serves a dual purpose in that it registers not only changes in Keithy, but changes in them as well. As Keithy struggles with his love for Diana, the coldness with which Diana meets everyone begins to change; but Keithy's love for Diana is a thing of annoyance for Patrick, and he reacts by becoming more irascible and intolerant. And finally, as we have already observed, Keithy is characterized by his love for his animals and by his participation in nature.

Stow gives Keithy the mental ability to learn and, within his limitation, to grow; and it is the writer's sympathy with Keithy's passage from innocence into experience and the delicacy with which he treats this change that make Keithy such an appealing character. Consider the scene in which Keithy, permitted to go to town with neighbor boys, is sent by the underage boys into a bar to buy beer. His lack of experience brings about the pain of humiliation.

He came over to the bar and said, as slowly and carefully as John had done: "Give me four bottles of beer."

"Cold?" asked the bartender.

All Keithy's confidence crumbled before the one unscripted question. He stared at the man and asked softly:

"What?"

"Cold?"

"No," he said, nervous now and bewildered. "I've got my jumper on."

The bartender took a look at his earnest face and raised his eyes to heaven. The customer laughed. The bartender went away grinning and came back with four warm bottles. (112)

Keithy is asked if he can pay for the beer and in response hands the bartender too much money. The man asks:

"Like some change?" asked the bartender.

"What?"

"Change. This stuff. You come right over here and I'll put it in your pocket for you."

At the lowest depths of humiliation, Keithy considered swinging at the man with two bottles of beer and flattening him, but he could never have done it. (112)

Later on the same day the Robson boys stop their car to pick up a couple of girls, "Peg and Bitcho," as Derek Robson calls them. One of the girls, to spite Derek, sits in Keithy's lap and begins to tease him. When Keithy does not respond to her caresses, she begins to move around on his lap, trying to arouse him sexually.

And then, at last, as she thought he was succumbing to her charms, he found out what she was doing.

His voice was thick with disgust. "Get out."

"Not at all?"

"Get out!" he shouted. "You're dirty." (116)

Keithy sits alone thinking, while the Robson boys take the girls away from the car.

But he was not thinking of them, he was remembering the day when he carried Diana across the road at Malin, when he had tried to kiss her and she had run away.

. . .

When you did that to a girl, tried to get close to her and feel her warmth against you and kiss her on the mouth, that was what she would think of you — what he had just thought of the dirty girl with red hair.
And so Keithy Farnham, until the day he died, never again openly touched or caressed or made any physical sign to the woman he loved. (117)

Keithy can learn, but as this scene illustrates — and as do others, such as his putting into application his learning of the word *ordeal* — both his experience and his reasoning ability are so limited that, instead of coming to truth, he replaces one degree of ignorance for another, and herein lies the pathos.

Stow's conception of Keithy and his execution of that conception do not require the technical innovation that has been required of other writers who have worked through a half-wit, such as Faulkner, for example; what it does require is a treatment that is objective as opposed to sentimental, yet sympathetic enough to keep the reader concerned, for it is on Keithy and his problems that the weight of the narrative rests. Stow succeeds in balancing sentiment and objectivity, and Keithy comes off as one of his finest creations.

With Diana and Patrick, Stow is not quite as successful. One has the feeling with Patrick that Stow is always looking at him, and almost never within him. For the most part, Patrick's characterization is dealt with in a narrative summary early in the novel. Though he is presented dramatically often enough in the latter half of the novel as he argues with Diana and with Keithy, as a character he seems static, changing little, remaining for the most part the literary offspring of the blended personalities of his parents in *A Haunted Land*. Stow tells us that he is lonely; that he is lame; that he is embittered by his past; that he has had illicit affairs; that he desperately wants a son and marries Diana for that reason. But we never see into Patrick's being. Why has he not married before now? He has money, land, houses, a cousin Nakala who has wanted to

marry him for years. He is, we learn from Diana, attractive. Why
has he remained lonely and miserable so long, only to come out of
this forty-five year habit with Diana, a woman who seems to
possess little humor or insight or love or charm, nothing more than
a kind of cold beauty? None of these questions are sufficiently
dealt with, nor is it made clear why Patrick cannot have the
patience with Diana that she requires.

Stow describes Patrick rummaging among the old photographs
and bric-a-brac from Malin and Koolabye — among memories of
the Maguires and the Leightons — having decided, it seems, to let
the past and its weight upon Patrick give the needed substance to
his characterization. But since Patrick is essentially the same person
at the end of the novel as he was at the beginning, this initial characterization by extension is not enough. While he is not exactly a
"flat" character, he is wooden, and for this reason the reader can
never come to a feeling of intimacy with him that he can even with
minor characters such as cousin Nakala or Patrick's house-man,
Fred.

Although Stow does have some difficulty with the characterization of Diana, he does a much better job with her than with
Patrick. In her identification with Keithy, in her learning to love
through him, she does change; and she is not the same locked-in
woman at the end of the novel as she is in the beginning. It seems to
me that P. H. Newby is quite wrong in writing that:

The denial of sex is what Keithy and Diana have in common and the defi-
ciency of the book is that no way of growth out of this sterility is indicated.
Mr. Stow is interested in frigidity as a literary situation, but he is unable to
develop it dramatically and, as frequently happens when a book lacks real
psychological development, it is brought to an end by the violent death of
one of the protagonists.[3]

Keithy's experience with "Bitcho" does teach him that sex is dirty,
but not love; and his final thrusting of himself into the woods to
prove his love for Diana seems to indicate a continued growth on
his part, regardless of his lack of intelligent understanding. To say
that Stow kills Keithy off because there is no psychological
development and he does not know what else to do with him is non-
sense. Diana's concentration camp experiences have also taught her
that sex is dirty; but before Patrick with his savage sarcasm makes

it impossible for her to feel secure enough with him for sexual intimacy, she does attempt to overcome her frigidity. One night in the
midst of a storm Diana comes to Patrick's bedroom. She tries to be
tender with him, but he puts her off. She asks:

> "Why cannot you love me the same way I love you?"
> "Listen, sweetheart, let's talk about horses. I've had enough of that
> particular subject."
> "Are you so hard? Are you all body and no heart?"
> He burst out then, losing his labored good humor.... (173)

Against his continued criticism, Diana reaches out to him and the
scene closes with the two of them spending the remainder of the
night together. In the chapters that follow, one gathers that the
night has not solved their problems, but Diana does struggle to
bring them together, until Patrick makes it no longer possible. In
light of Diana's attempts, I fail to understand Newby's charge that
Stow does not develop the problem of frigidity dramatically. There
are numerous scenes that prove wrong Newby's charge that Diana
does not grow out of sexual sterility, but even more important are
those scenes that show Diana finally able to love, both Patrick,
until he kills her love, and Keithy. It seems to me that Diana's final
decision to return to Lingarin to care for Keithy until his parents
return is more than a selfish way out of her problem with Patrick,
and is a clear indication of her growth and change.

Stow's only real problem with Diana is similar to his problem
with Patrick. He is not as successful as he might be in the rendering
of her inward self, her thoughts. With Patrick he doesn't often
make an effort; with Diana the effort is made frequently, but the
result is sometimes hollow and the diction stilted. About this problem Leonie Kramer writes that Stow "is able to transmit only the
mechanical click of her internal monologue."[4] To make her point,
she quotes the following passage:

> Admit then, admit, now you are alone, that you have lied and stolen
> from him. Admit that you deceived him for what he had and you had not,
> a place for ever. Confess your guilt, it is time now.
> But say, too, that you have loved him, as you can love, who have
> learned young to hate the rot in the soul of animal man. Say that you loved
> him with a love older and stronger than his, though he wounds you for it.
> And for that love, what has he given you? Oh hurt and hurt, opening old

scars with his bitter words, with his angers and suspicions. In what way
have I freed myself when he imprisons me so?
      Go then. It is ended. Go and hide, as you have hidden before in the
nameless crowd. That is the only freedom you may have. (212)

Stow has Diana, for whom English is not a native language,
speak in the formal, often stilted manner of a foreigner; but even
making this allowance, the above passage is still filled with emotional clichés. This lapse on Stow's part does not happen frequently; but it does happen, and it happens in all his novels, particularly in scenes when one character is trying to express love for
another. The dialogue in these scenes often reads as though Stow is
embarrassed by the necessity of a face-to-face expression of emotion. Such lapses are curious for a writer whose prose is usually
excellent, and because the reader is accustomed to such a high standard on Stow's part, the slips are even more apparent when they
come.
      And yet, it seems that Kramer is being too hard on Stow when
she writes: "Diana Ravirs does not ring true; she engages no sympathy and attracts no censure."[5] While I agree with Kramer in seeing no reason for censure, I find, as the numerous quoted passages
regarding Diana and Keithy indicate, ample possibility for sympathy. It is true that Stow's initial images projecting Diana are
associated with coldness, i.e., "ice," "iceberg," "frozen," and
through much of the novel Diana does "ring true" to these images;
but she also warms up, "thaws," if you will, as she participates in
Keithy's warmth and love.
      With the minor characters in *The Bystander,* particularly Nakala
and Fred, Stow is quite successful. Nakala, like Patrick, is a descen-
dant from Stow's first novel. Yet, with a few swift touches Stow
brings the mannish, motorcycle riding, acid-tongued Nakala to life
more fully than he ever does Patrick. Like Fred, Nakala is both an
individual and a representative Australian type. It is the cranky
Fred who later refuses to take orders from Diana when she moves
to Koolabye and thus deepens the quarrel between Diana and
Patrick; and it is Fred who kills Keithy's snake and brings further
trouble between Keithy and Patrick. Always true to his nature,
Fred is second only to Keithy in being the finest characterization in
the novel.
      Other characters — the Farnhams, a particularly silly lady psy-

chologist who talks to Keithy, and the Robsons who take Keithy to town — are also well drawn, and in terms of characterization, Stow is far less vulnerable to criticism in *The Bystander* than in *A Haunted Land.*

III *Structure*

The structure of *The Bystander* is also quite different from that of *A Haunted Land.* For one thing, Stow's cast of characters is smaller and there is not the need to dispose of them as he does in the first novel, so whereas a basic part of the structure of *A Haunted Land* depends on the dramatic exits of the characters, exits often accompanied by displays of temperament or violence, the structure of *The Bystander* is formed around the internal changes in the three major characters and the manner in which the individual's change affects the other two. *A Haunted Land* begins some fifty years after the main action, then flashes back to ten years before the main action, then takes up the story proper. There is no such manipulation in *The Bystander.* Diana arrives; Keithy comes to love her; she marries Patrick; the marriage fails; she decides to return to Lingarin and keep Keithy; the woods burn and we are at the climax of the novel as Keithy runs into the conflagration for his ordeal. Although in *The Bystander* there is some relationship between a character's attitude and the seasons, and although one particular scene is played against the background of a storm, neither the seasons nor the weather play any significant part in the novel's structure, as they did in *A Haunted Land.* Stow does restrict his time span to within a year as he did in the first novel, but the reader is not made as aware of the passing of time in this novel, and structurally it is not of any particular importance.

The design of *The Bystander* is a scenic one, and the scenes are so clearly set off that they will bear labeling: Diana arrives; Diana meets Keithy; Diana alone; Diana and Patrick; Diana and Keithy and Patrick; etc. Interspersed among the major scenes are the minor ones: Nakala alone; Nakala and Patrick; Keithy in town; Patrick and Fred at Koolabye; etc. Since the action is less frantic in *The Bystander* than in *A Haunted Land,* and since Stow is most interested in the psychological interplay of his characters, his design for the novel is an effective one. In a subtle way the clarity of the design and leisurely pace of the action reflect the spacious-

ness of the setting; and it is in harmony with the honesty and sim-
plicity of Keithy, whose loving vision of reality permeates the
novel.

As the scenes change, so does the point of view; and Stow handles his omniscience so effectively that there is never the obvious-
ness of author control or manipulation that one sometimes finds
when the point of view is changed as often as it is in this novel. In
remarking on this aspect of the novel, Newby writes:

No doubt this style has come to Mr. Stow naturally, but if it hasn't then in
all probability he learned it from D. H. Lawrence. In the quick, lizard-like
manner he is in and out of the minds of a dozen people. He is clever with
conversation, using it for the weight of his narrative, which means that he
is dramatizing, dramatizing all the time. This is excellent, and as with
Lawrence, the first page or so of a chapter will be from the point of view
of one of the characters.[6]

Although Stow had not yet read Lawrence when he wrote *The Bystander,* there is a healthy similarity in their handling of point of
view, and Newby puts Stow in good company by indicating this.

IV   *Theme*

There are two ideas, or themes, that Stow is working with in *The
Bystander.* One, involving Keithy, is, as the title indicates, the problem of the bystander, as Keithy loses his place of security and
moves from the sidelines into participation, and with this into
involvement. With involvement comes experience, and the consequent loss of innocence. The initiation theme is, of course, as old as
writing itself and it is a theme that has been particularly popular
with twentieth century writers. What makes Stow's handling of the
theme different is the mental limitations of Keithy. A loss of innocence is particularly dangerous for Keithy. Patrick recognizes this,
saying, ''. . . if he grows up as much as that, if he starts wanting the
same things that normal people want — well, what'll happen to
him? What chance has he got to be happy that way? He'll just be a
deformity, and he'll know it before long'' (145).

Child of nature, surrounded by his animals and filled with an
innocent love and an innocent's understanding, a sexual awakening
is something he cannot handle, and the passage into experience is

overwhelmingly disastrous. Stow uses the initiation theme again in the last of his five novels, *The Merry-Go-Round in the Sea*, and again his understanding of the ways of a child is delicately transcribed, but it is the miscarried initiation of Keithy that will remain in the reader's memory long after the more normal initiation of Rob in *The Merry-Go-Round in the Sea* is forgotten.

The other major theme in the novel is one that Stow deals with in the first four of the five novels, and even to a certain extent in the last; it is a theme that Geoffrey Dutton treats extensively in his survey of Stow's work, the theme he identifies as "the search for permanence."[7] In *A Haunted Land* the theme can be seen in Andrew Maguire's attempts to keep Malin and his five children separate and whole unto himself. Through his pride and will he loses all, both his family and, finally, Malin, as after his death it too begins to decay.

In *The Bystander* all the characters are involved to one degree or another in a search for permanence. Keithy's mother must return to England where she feels her roots are. Patrick's man Fred fights Diana to stay at Koolabye where he belongs. Patrick's cousin Nakala complains to him, "I want to keep everything the same forever," and continues, "You don't have to be old to want to hold on to things. I'm not ancient ... but I couldn't bear a change at Strathmore. Sometimes I look at those hills and thank God that no one can do anything to them" (181).

The search for something to hold on to is a strong one for Diana, Patrick, and Keithy. On the second page of the novel Diana hears the lines from the hillbilly song "I don't want something for nothing, I just want something forever." When Keithy goes to town with the Robson boys, he hears the song in a record store and buys the record for Diana. Diana accepts the record with pleasure, only to have Keithy's mother remark, "The joke is ... that we haven't a gramophone" (119). Turning the record around and around in her hands, Diana remarks, "Who knows? Perhaps some day I will have a gramophone for myself" (119).

The irony here is typical of Stow's gentle touch, but beyond this is the projection of Diana's aims. She is out to get something forever; and it is this greed, made understandable because of her wartime treatment as a displaced person, that makes her look beyond Patrick as a person to Patrick as one who can give her things. The "something forever" to Diana is not perceived in terms of love (until Keithy she doesn't know what this is), but rather in terms of material possessions. At the end of the novel, Diana, leaving Patrick and coming to terms with herself, thinks: "Admit that you deceived him for what he had and you had not, a place for ever" (212).

Patrick is also looking for something forever. He marries Diana for a son, one through whom he can hold on to Koolabye and Malin. And when through her frigidity Diana denies him, Patrick can see her only in terms of one who has cheated him out of what he most wants. His need to hold on is seen clearly as he and Diana are talking in the aftermath of a storm that has blown down a huge Norfolk pine at Koolabye. Patrick says: "'God, I hate time. You can't keep anything safe from it. Not the tree, not Malin, not Koolabye. It took so much to build them, yet — someday I'll die; twenty or thirty years time, maybe, but that doesn't seem so far away — and then there they'll be, sold to a pastoral company or split up into little farms...'" (176).

For both Diana and Patrick the experiences of their past — the humiliation and denial of necessities for Diana, the illegitimacy and lameness for Patrick — produce in them an excessive pride and egotism. It is the same sort of destructive pride that Stow first deals with in Andrew Maguire in *A Haunted Land*. And as the uncompromising pride destroyed the relationship between Maguire and his family, so does it destroy any possible harmony between Patrick and Diana.

Keithy's need for permanence has nothing to do with tangible possessions, but rather with love. He needs Diana and he needs Patrick, but he needs them separate, for in his innocence he is wise enough to see that together they are both lost to him. The search for permanence, a particular kind of permanence, differs with each person, and it is a theme Stow is to work with again in the novels that follow *The Bystander*.

Since *A Haunted Land* and *The Bystander* are two different kinds of novels, the first a romance, the second a realistic novel, it is difficult to make an evaluative comparison between the two, particularly in terms of characterization and plot. Yet granting Stow his choice of forms and without a judgment of the form itself, it is possible to judge his accomplishment within the form, and, with this overview, it seems that he is far more successful in *The Bystander* than in *A Haunted Land*. In writing *The Bystander* as a realistic novel, Stow cannot allow himself the ease of making types stand for characters or having repeated violent action replace character development and change. For this reason the second novel demands of him a greater grasp of his characters and a closer attention to their motivation.

With the noted exceptions, Stow handles the challenge quite well. Yet he does not seem completely happy with realism; and in *To the Islands,* his third novel, we find him once again experimenting, this time attempting to form a hybrid that is neither quite romance nor quite realism.

CHAPTER 4

To the Islands

STOW'S third novel, *To the Islands,* gained him more critical attention than either of the first two. It was published in England, America, Germany, and Australia, in that order, and in Australia it won the Book of the Year Award and the Miles Franklin Award. Representative of the initial praise the novel received is the following quotation from Granville Hicks, who, describing the novel in *The Saturday Review,* wrote:

Stow's perceptions are deep and true, and he has miraculously found the way to communicate what he understands. His style, never merely pretty and never lush, is truly poetic and perfectly suited to his theme. Universal is a large word, but if it can ever be used it can be applied to *To the Islands,* which reaches down to the basic stratum of human nature.[1]

In Australia critics were quick to point approvingly to Stow as a disciple of Patrick White, who the year before (1957) had published *Voss,* a novel whose protagonist, a nineteenth century explorer named Voss, makes a trip across the outback, a journey of geographical exploration that becomes at the same time an inward journey of spiritual quest. Australian critics were particularly happy with Stow, for the novel, added with White's *Voss* and an earlier novel, *The Tree of Man,* seemed to indicate a trend away from the traditional Australian novel, one grounded in realism and humanism. It suggested a movement toward a more complex interior fiction, one thematically concerned with man's spiritual nature and presented either in terms of symbol and myth or psychological analysis. Time has proven the critics correct, for there have been other novels — by such writers as Elizabeth Harrower, Thea Astley, and Thomas Keneally — and another novel, *Tourmaline,* by Stow, to illustrate a widening concern in the area early dealt with by Patrick White.

Not all critics viewed *To the Islands* with equal enthusiasm, how-ever. And from a standpoint of both distance and time, the original cries of praise for Stow's venture into symbolism and allegory seem less trustworthy than those dissenting voices that indicated the shortcomings of the novel, voices such as that of Leonie Kramer, who, while admiring the novel as an experiment, pointed to Stow's gift for realism as the aspect of the novel most deserving of praise.[2]

Coming to *To the Islands* in a chronological treatment of Stow's fiction such as this one, it would satisfy one's sense of order to be able to say that Stow begins with a romance in *A Haunted Land,* finds his voice in the poetic realism of *The Bystander,* and perfects that voice in his third novel, *To the Islands.* Yet such is not the case, for the pattern that does emerge is not one of linear development, but rather one of convolution and experimentation. As Andrew Maguire in *A Haunted Land* was less real than the setting he domi-nated, so is the missionary Heriot in *To the Islands.* But whereas in Maguire Stow created a character only suggestive of the mythic, the allegorical, he creates in Heriot a character who must be seen in terms of the allegorical in order for the story to carry the intended meaning. Yet Stow presents Heriot and his developing story in a curious way. Stow is not writing a romance as in *A Haunted Land,* nor is he writing a story of straightforward allegory, for the first third of the novel is presented in a realistic manner analogous to the presentation of *The Bystander.* However, at a point approximately one-third of the way through the novel, Heriot becomes, as Stow would have us view him, a kind of Everyman, whose journey across the vast northwestern Australian wilderness is a representative journey of man in search of his soul. In his mixture of realism and allegory, and in his efforts to delineate the mental processes of Heriot, Stow sets for himself an ambitious task, one presenting problems that he is not able to handle successfully. The problems are serious ones, and I want to deal with them at length, but in order to provide a framework for that discussion, a brief summary of the plot will be useful.

I *Plot*

The setting for the novel is the wilderness area of the Kimberley Mountains in northwestern Australia. The action takes place first at an isolated Christian mission where a small number of whites are attempting to care for and to "civilize" a small number of aborigines. The setting in the second two-thirds of the novel moves through the ever-expanding outback, a land of mountains and desert and infinite space.

The protagonist, Heriot, is an old man at sixty-seven, who, with his white hair and white beard and stern demeanor, is a patriarch both in appearance and in terms of the hold he has over the natives. He is the last of the old school missionaries who converted with a whip and disciplined with a vengeance.

As the novel begins, Heriot is a bitter man, self-rebuking, lonely, tired. Stow writes:

Heriot sat up and lowered his feet to the floor, slow in all his movements under the weight of his years and tiredness. Walking to the shower, his feet brushed the ground, his head was bent and his eyes lowered from the wounding light. Yet he was a tall man, stooping there under the overhanging thatch, a big man with his wild white hair, his face carved and calm. The lizards scattered from his path, the crows cried. . . .[3]

Looking at himself in a cracked mirror, Heriot

. . . saw himself as a great red cliff, rising from the rocks of his own ruin. I am an old man. *J'ai plus de souvenirs que si j'avais mille ans,* and this cursed Baudelaire whining in his head like a mosquito, preaching despair. How does a man grow old who has made no investment in the future, without wife or child, without refuge for his heart beyond the work that becomes too much for him?

Because his despair grew on the cracked face in the cracked glass he turned away and finished dressing. (13)

The mission nurse, watching Heriot in the chapel at prayer, wonders: "What does he say, morning after morning, kneeling up so straightly. How does he go on year after year, with always the same day ahead of him. Is it the prayer itself that gives him strength?" (18).

The Heriot who appears strong to the natives who both fear and love him, strong to the whites who both respect and resent him, is strong in will, is strong in resentment, but tremulous in spirit, in faith, in hope. In talking to the mission preacher, Heriot says of himself, complaining of his projected death:

"And after all these years of being forgotten and ignored I suddenly find that I resent it. I don't want to pass piously to quiet grave. I've built something nobody wanted, and now the thing I think would give my life its full meaninglessness would be to smash it down and take it with me. Let them regret it when it's not there if they won't appreciate it when it is." (74)

To demonstrate his feelings, Heriot takes up an ivory crucifix and smashes it. " 'I believe in nothing,' Heriot said softly. 'I can pull down the world' " (78).

Heriot has asked to be relieved of his post as director of the mission, but a replacement cannot be found; and Stow in the first third of the novel shows Heriot impatiently waiting, dealing with the childlike aborigines, with the cluster of whites, some of whom dislike him. The turning point of the novel comes with the return of the native Rex to the mission. Rex has been married to Esther, the aboriginal girl Heriot and his now dead wife raised as their own child. The girl has died after her marriage to Rex, presumably because of his abuse. Heriot has held Rex responsible and has hated him and kept him away from the mission. He now refuses to allow Rex to remain, and Rex, playing the other blacks against Heriot, tries to overcome Heriot's authority over the natives.

The showdown between the angry Heriot and the stubborn Rex comes one dark noon, as a gathering cyclone breaks and begins to beat down upon the mission. Heriot, stopping to look at a piece of tin about to be blown loose from a building under construction, sees Rex and again demands that he leave the mission.

The wind was reaching its peak, filling the air not only with dust but also with leaves and grass, tearing down branches. The loose sheet of iron clattered on the roof, a continual assault on his nerves. He walked with his head down, his hair tormented into white wisps.

Then on the calf of his leg came an enormous impact, a great numbing pain. He swung round, looking down, and found what he had half known would be there. The first stone.

The first stone. And across huge desolations towered the figure of Rex, appearing and disappearing through a curtain of dust, his teeth showing in an uncertain grin.

Heriot bent down and took the stone in his hand, heavy, lethal. He was the martyr, struck by the first instrument of execution. The air was full of faces and raised hands. Walking towards Rex he was stumbling through murdering crowds, buffeted with screaming, spat on and wounded. And before all was one face, the dark face with its frozen white grin above the white shirt.

But he would be no martyr, not submit to these flailings as if owning himself wrong, he would strike back, godlike; not he, but the fierce crowd would die.

He sobbed in his throat. The stone flew. (78)

The tin flies from the building; the air is filled with dust; Heriot stands over the fallen Rex and thinks him dead.

Before the storm abates, Heriot in a trancelike state takes a gun from his room and with no provisions is ready to go into the wilderness, presumably to take his life. He is stopped by his aborigine friend Justin, who is aware that Heriot means to do himself harm.

"Nandaba grambun?" Justin asked placatingly. "Where are you going?"

Slowly Heriot swung into the saddle and towered there with the rifle before him, his shirt and his hair fluttering, but himself as still as a ship's figurehead set on a flinching horse nervous at the ears. He said sadly from the sky: "Mudumudu-gu ngurambum, abula."

"Ah, brother," Justin murmured, not smiling, "you got those islands on the brain." (88)

"Those islands" refers to the islands beyond the mountains, beyond the desert, islands in the sea where the aborigines believe the dead go. The legendary islands, so expected and so feared by the natives, have been a part of Heriot's mission life; and though on a practical level he does not believe in their existence, they become now as symbolically important for him as they are real for the natives. He has killed Rex, he believes; and now he must die, either by his own hand, with his gun, or by the wastes that will surely kill him if he fails to do so himself. What Heriot does not anticipate is that Justin in his faithfulness will not allow him to go alone. And so, against Heriot's will, Justin, who carries blankets and food, sets out with Heriot into the wilderness.

Justin says:

"Brother —"

They stared hungrily at one another. "Yes?"

"If you go along with me, I go with you, always."

Beyond the uneasy trees rose the hills, and beyond them again the country of the lost, huge wilderness between his last haunt of civilization and the unpeopled sea.

"Welcome, my Good Deeds," whispered Heriot. "Now I hear thy voice, I weep for very sweetness of love." (82–83)

The remaining two-thirds of the novel is primarily concerned with the journey of Heriot and Justin, although there are scenes that return the reader to the mission, where preparations are made to search for Heriot, as well as scenes involving the search party. There is also a brief love development between the nurse and a mission worker, which in the working out of the plot and theme is insignificant. Once Heriot has left, the only real importance of the mission scenes is in nurse Helen's discussion with the recuperating Rex of what Heriot has done to him and why, and her discussion with another mission worker of the importance of the mission effort and the responsibility of the white man to the black man.

The trip occurs simultaneously on two levels, the first exterior, as Stow realistically records the journey of the two men; the second interior, as Heriot travels from self-hate to peace. On the realistic level, Stow takes Heriot past blue hills, past blue pools, past spreading fields of damp grass, across the plains, and finally up into the red rock mountains and onto the cliffs overlooking the sea. Along the way Heriot meets a group of withered naked aborigines camped at the foot of a mountain, waiting for death. He meets an old prospector who has killed his partner years before and is wandering about the wilderness in expiation for his sins, much as Heriot himself is wandering. He meets also another old man, the only human remaining at a deserted mission; the two talk of the hardness of life, and Heriot explains how he came to be a missionary.

Heriot and Justin continue to make their way toward the sea. But one stop remains. "He [Heriot] was almost asleep when they came, after hours, to the country of caves, where bluffs and cliffs of rock were split with dark holes, and where, green and luxuriant, a glea tree reached out from among the boulders" (191–92). Because there is water, Justin, who throughout the long wandering journey has cared for Heriot as though he were a child, decides that they will camp near the caves. Stow writes of Heriot:

Long afterwards he got to his feet again and walked towards the mouth of the cave close by the pond. And under hanging rock he saw the first of the paintings, the crude figure of a man without a mouth, his head outlined with a horseshoe shape like that of the rainbow serpent.

"I know you," he said. "You are Wolaro. God. What does it matter what you are called." (192)

Heriot and Justin talk about death, the possibility of reincarnation, of the spirit living on in the remembrance of those who are living. Heriot no longer yearns for death, but he does long to be alone with his thoughts, with the bones and the cave drawings. He asks Justin to leave him; and Justin, knowing he has served Heriot as well as he can, leaves the old man alone. Some time later he encounters the search party, which includes, at his own insistence, Rex, who in part is transformed through Heriot's fall from grace on his account.

Heriot spends his final days in a kind of dream state. "In the dimness of the cave, days ran together and lost themselves, so that Heriot, sleeping, eating, or disjointedly thinking, felt time confounded, a twilight without divisions, and himself a simple plant of the sea's floor, wavering and dying" (200). On the third day Heriot leaves the cave and begins the final stumbling movement toward the sea. He passes a night, and at the next day at sunrise,

He came forward to the edge of the cliffs, where they dropped, vast red walls, to the faraway sea below. And the sea, where the light was not on it, was the blue-green of opals and endlessly rearing, smashed into white at the foot of the rock.

There was a break in the cliffs, and he climbed unsteadily down a few yards to a red ledge with a cave behind it. The skulls were there again, the eyes of the mouthless god, turned forever towards the islands. But the islands — the islands. He stared out to the sea and saw nothing but the sun on the water; his dreams and his fears all true, and there were no islands. (203)

He stands poised on the edge of the sea, waiting, watching:

High overhead the eagle patrolled the cliff. But suddenly, passing under it, a gull flew out from the rock and planed towards the sun until it was hidden in light. And when the sun sank lower, there in the heart of the blaze, might appear the islands.

The old man knelt among the bones and stared into the light. His carved lips were firm in the white beard, his hands were steady, his ancient blue eyes, neither hoping nor fearing, searched sun and sea for the least dark hint of a landfall.

"My soul," he whispered, over the seasurge, "my soul is a strange country." (203-204)

II *Heriot: Problems in Characterization*

Reduced to its simplest level, *To the Islands* is about a tired and bitter old man who feels himself a failure, who in anger strikes another, and who, in a state of confusion, wanders through the wilderness mulling over his deed, until arriving at the sea, he lies down and dies. This is the surface level, the realistic level of the novel. The major problem in the novel comes from Stow's clear intention that the novel have more than a surface meaning, that it do more than tell a story. Yet, he seems uncertain as to just what sort of novel he is writing, and because he never reaches a clear conception of a level of presentation in the story, his presentation wanders between realism and the mythopoetic; and, for the reader, the result is confsion or ambivalence concerning how he is to view the major character, Heriot.

In his Preface to the novel, Stow writes: "This is not, by intention, a realistic novel; no white character, therefore, and no major incident in the plot is drawn from life" (ix). In the second paragraph of the Preface, he states:

The country crossed by Heriot was suggested by the North Kimberley, but as this has been crossed by few white men, myself not among them, it is an extension of the region in which I lived for a short time rather than the route of an actual journey. I have however consulted C. Price Conigrave's autobiography *Walkabout* (Dent, 1938) with its account of his explorations of over forty years ago, and believe that Heriot's travels are more accurate, topographically, than was strictly necessary to the plot. (ix)

We are asked, then, in the Preface, to view the novel simultaneously on two levels: an antirealistic creation of the poet's imagination, and at the same time a realistically recreated setting through which we are to be aware of our movement. This dual presentation need not necessarily make a problem for Stow, as long as he is consistent: real setting; plus characters conceived along the lines of the symbolic, or the allegorical, or the mythopoetic, however he originally sees them. The problem that does arise is that Stow is not consistent, for while the minor characters are always treated on a realistic level, even though they are not developed as fully as they might be, the major characters, Heriot and Justin, and particularly Heriot, are both real and then suddenly symbolic, with their journey through the wilderness rising into allegory.

The reader does not easily make the shift in viewpoint, not because such a shift is impossible, but because Stow has not prepared the reader for the shift. As one critic sees the problem, "[The] third novel is unhappily situated in a no man's land between symbolic and mundane reality, and it is difficult for the reader to yield to it in the way that is obviously required of him."[4]

A writer in deciding to create allegorical figures can move from either of two points of departure. He can begin with characters who are types — for example, a rather fully realized type such as Hester Prynne, or a transparent figure such as Everyman (who is quoted by Heriot) — or else he can create a character of flesh and blood whose action, because it is representative, i.e., universal, can be seen in allegorical terms — such as Jay Gatsby, a kind of American Everyman, or Ike McCaslin. Stow, with a realistic setting, real aborigines, and real minor white characters, creates a real protagonist, Heriot. Although Heriot is not adequately developed, he is realistically treated, as early in the novel he ministers to the aborigines and participates in the workings of the mission. Stow's problem comes when he attempts to make Heriot universal, when he tries to make Heriot's journey from the mission to the sea Everyman's journey, his psychic journey from his dark night of the soul to peace and harmony a representative journey.

Stow fails with Heriot because he does not do enough work with him at this point to make him sufficiently real for the reader. He comes across as a Hester Prynne in a situation that calls for a character even more fully delineated than a Jay Gatsby. He is a surface character, a character the reader looks *at* rather than into. While Stow can make do with such a rendering in Patrick Leighton in *The Bystander,* he cannot make Heriot a "flat" character, because it is on Heriot and his motivation, his changes from hate to love, from singularity to unity, that the meaning of the novel depends. In order for the reader to be able to identify with Heriot as he struggles and as he changes — i.e., in order for his problems and the resultant journey and acceptance to be raised to the universal level that allegory demands — the reader must be privy to and participate in Heriot's mental struggles. The struggles must not only be suggested, but they must also be shown. Stow does not make such a participation possible, again because he does not present Heriot in sufficient depth.

It seems to me that Leonie Kramer is quite wrong when she writes, in defense of Stow: "In choosing to write an anti-realistic novel, he is of course in one sense immediately relieved of the burden of imposing some order and consistency upon human behavior. Character becomes a function of plot, and more particularly of symbolism; it need not, indeed cannot, be explored *per se*."[5] Kramer is wrong because the term "anti-realistic" cannot be made to fit *To the Islands,* for this is not the kind of novel Stow has written.

Several critics, without analyzing the problem, do comment on it. David Martin indicates one way of seeing the flaw in Heriot by writing: "...the symbolism does not flow from character and action, but character and action are vessels to hold a symbolism."[6] George Johnston, writing about the same problem, says:

The whole novel stands or fails by the figure of Heriot, which is supposed to be charged with reverberating significance: he is Lear; he is Don Quixote; he is, at last, Everyman. If Heriot is not all of us, he is nothing, merely a crazy mission manager. Some critics have granted Mr. Stow his effect of universality. I would not, because to me Heriot's significance is merely heavily insisted on, not achieved....[7]

Both of these critics see the novel, as I see it, as a work which is essentially realistic, and because it is this sort of novel, certain demands are made of Heriot, demands which Stow does not meet.

As he introduces Heriot, Stow uses a device of character delineation that provides vagueness rather than depth. When dealing with Heriot, Stow often becomes poetic, either in his own descriptive language raised to poetry or in having Heriot quote lines from numerous writers, often in a language other than English. The first two paragraphs of the novel illustrate this characteristic:

A child dragged a stick along the corrugated iron wall of a hut, and Heriot woke and found the morning standing at his bed like a valet, holding out his daylight self to be put on again, his name, his age, his vague and wearying occupation. His eyes, not yet broken to the light, rested on the mud-brick wall beside his bed, drifted slowly upwards to the grass-thatched roof. From a rafter an organ-grinder lizard peered sidelong over its pulsing throat.

Collecting himself from sleep, returning to his life, he said to the lizard: "I am Heriot. This is the sixty-seventh year of my age. *Rien n'égale en longueur les boiteuses journees* —" (1)

"A child dragged a stick along the corrugated iron wall of a hut," "the mud-brick wall," a peering lizard; these carefully recorded realistic details are typical of Stow's style throughout the novel: as he deals with the mission, the aborigines, the old men Heriot meets on his journey, the journey itself; and yet, with Heriot, he often changes his level of language and the result is something like "the morning standing by his bed like a valet, holding out his daylight self to be put on again," and the quotation, *"Rien n'égale en longueur les boiteuses journees."*

Leonie Kramer, using this same passage as an example, writes:

> Stow has two voices. The one is precise, carefully modulated, and speaks with modesty and persuasiveness. The other is less reliable; sometimes it is given to hollow declamation, sometimes to self-conscious rhetoric. [Here Kramer quotes the above passage.]
> There one is directly confronted with the curiously schizophrenic quality of Stow's writing. Simple, telling detail turns into grandiose, and in this case slightly ludicrous metaphor. [8]

Kramer is accurate in her judgment, but what she might have further indicated is that Stow resorts to this kind of rhetoric only in those instances when he is struggling with characterization. This is seen in his first novel, and it is seen particularly in this novel in relation to Heriot. The purpose of the quotations, the literary allusions, varies; but generally the purpose seems to be to add substance to Heriot, by reinforcing either an observation Stow has made about him or one he has made about himself:

> He saw himself as a great red cliff, rising from the rocks of his own ruin. I am an old man, an old man, *J'ai plus de souvenirs que si j'avais mille ans.* (13)

Or to deepen his characterization by suggesting a man of insight:

Heriot, seated beside the [radio] set with a pad in front of him, sketched a crumbling cliff with the profile of the Sphinx. "And I am Ozymandias, king of kings," he said. "Too old to be so weak, such a self-pitying fool." (13)

With a violent gust the wind threw up a white curtain. Rex was gone, vanished in a shroud of dust. Around him Heriot believed he saw dark figures struggling towards him in a dry mist. "Why, this is hell," he whispered, "why, this is hell, nor am I out of it." (79)

or to indicate Heriot to be a learned man with a philosophically speculative nature:

And the cursed Baudelaire whining in his head like a mosquito, preaching despair. How does a man grow old who has made no investment in the future, without wife or child, without refuge for his heart beyond the work that becomes too much for him. (13)

In the first three instances the quotations intrude because they take the reader away from the isolated Australian mission and into the world of literary allusion. The last fails, as do the others finally, because Stow never gives us enough background to suggest how Heriot came to such a fund of literary associations. Little of his past is known, his education, his aspirations, how he has spent his private time. The result is that the quotations seem to drop from the air, or from an obtrusive author, and not from the genuineness of Heriot.[9]

Stow makes further use of the quotation as a short-cut method of "telling" rather than "showing," or suggesting by allusion rather than by particular dramatization of Heriot's mental states. For example, as Heriot and Justin go further into the wilderness, Heriot's fear of the vast blankness that lies before him is revealed in a single line, *"Le silence éternal de ces espaces infines m'efraie"* (100). How much more successful is Stow when on those infrequent occasions he finds his "objective correlative." To show Heriot's reaction to the land, Stow at another point writes: "Coming down the hillside, seeing, instead of rock, spreading grasslands patched here and there with blue pools and with gum trees, cadjiputs and lonely baobabs, Heriot sighed and felt peace rise like a wind from the plain" (108). Yet, this kind of character revelation is exceptional. Heriot's spiritual struggle, for example, is often made no more personal, no more dramatic than through his repetition of a memorized prayer.

In the instances when Stow does dramatize Heriot's feelings, the result is often superficial, more melodramatic than convincing, for the narrator has the reader looking at Heriot from the outside as he is reacting, rather than showing the workings of his mind.

III   *Heriot's Motivation*

Not only is Stow's failure to adequately dramatize Heriot's spiritual struggle a serious shortcoming in the novel, but an equal, if not greater flaw is his failure to adequately illustrate Heriot's motivation. There are questions unanswered from the beginning of the novel. What is the cause of Heriot's malaise, and how is it more than the general malaise that comes to anyone? Buckley, on this point, writes of *To the Islands:* "Although more sophisticated in its workings than *A Haunted Land,* it is also more compulsive. Andrew maguire's madness was noted, gradually revealed, analyzed and (almost) accounted for; but Heriot's desolation is not. It is played on rather than defined, is a motif rather than a subject."[10]

Other questions arise. Why, before his confrontation with Rex, is it so necessary for Heriot to leave the mission? And how has hatred so overcome him that he throws a stone in vengeance at Rex? The given motivation — that Rex has destroyed Heriot's adopted daughter — does not, considering the time that has passed, suggest sufficient cause for Heriot's uncontrolled rage.

Perhaps even more important than these unanswered questions are those surrounding Heriot's trek through the wilderness. How does he change from an old man who seeks death to an old man who seeks life, from one who hates to one who loves? For example, on the first day of the journey Heriot wants to kill himself and is angry that Justin prevents it. Before night falls, Heriot stares at the sky:

Four brolgas, attenuated and grey, crossed the sky with a long purring crake like the opening of an old door. Heriot sat up.
  "What are you thinking?" he demanded.
  "Nothing."
  "Damn you, damn you, damn you," whispered Heriot to the sky. "You do me wrong, you do me wrong to take me out of the grave." (102)

The next morning, with no given reason for Heriot's change, Stow writes:

> In the morning Heriot woke happy, light filled the gorge and reached his bones, he felt careless and at ease. Justin at the fire, grilling his fish, looked up warily and saw the white man's face, and smiled, whitely and warmly. "You are feeling good again," he said.
>
> "Very good," said Heriot, squatting beside him. . . . (102)

What is missing here is some sort of explanation for Heriot's change, and one wonders why, since Stow did so well with Keithy's emotions in *The Bystander,* he does not do a similar explanation of Heriot's change in terms of the effect the land has on him, especially since he does later recount Heriot's sensitivity to the beauty of the wilderness. But here nothing of this is suggested.

Some fifty pages later, writing a series of scenes in which Heriot is talking with Rusty, the old prospector who has murdered his partner, Stow records Heriot's thinking on his supposed murder of Rex and why he must go on. The episode itself is a vague one, like Heriot's later encounter in which he philosophizes emptily with the old man at the abandoned mission. Yet the purpose of the episode is to bring Heriot to a degree of self-realization, and thus provide a motivation for his continuing to live and his continuing to the islands.

Reflecting silently on aspects of Rex's life, Heriot announces to Rusty,

> "Now I know," he said from a great distance, "I know why I'm going on."
>
> "Why's that?" asked the man, soft as canegrass in the wind.
>
> "Because all this time I've been deceiving myself. Telling myself I was old and weak, and I'm not. Telling myself I wanted to die, but I don't, no, and I never will. All this has been self-pity, nothing else." (155)

Heriot, philosophizing on his nature, discusses inherited sin.

> He scrubbed his forehead with a brown fist. "Now I remember — the things I used to know."
>
> "What?" asked the man, still intently watching. "What did you know?"
>
> "About crimes. About being born out of crimes. It was because of mur-

ders that I was ever born in this country. It was because of murders my first amoebic ancestor ever survived to be my ancestor. Every day in my life murders are done to protect me. People are taught how to murder because of me. Oh, God," said Heriot savagely, "if there was a God this filthy Australian, British, human blood would have been dried up in me with a thunderbolt when I was born."

"You can't help being born, mate."

"I'm glad to have been born now. This is a good time for it, with the world dying. The crimes have mounted up now, we can sit and enjoy the stink of our own rot." (155–56)

Slightly melodramatic, slightly pompous, this speech of Heriot's is representative of the way Stow handles Heriot throughout the novel. Although motivation is accounted for here, because of the particular tone the passage takes the motivation sounds a bit hollow. Consider a similar explanation of motivation, one which contains all Stow gives one about Heriot's overall motivation. In explaining to the old man at the abandoned mission why he became a missionary, Heriot says:

"Expiation," . . . . "Yes. This is my third life."

"What was the others?" asked Sam incuriously.

"I suppose it was my birth, as a human being, that drove me to charity. Yes, that was the first. And then there was the massacre, done by my race at Onmalmeri."

"I heard of it," said Sam.

"That was the second. It drove me to the mission. And then at the end there was my — my hatred."

"What'd that drive you to?" murmured Sam.

"That?" said Heriot pensively. "That has made a lost man of me."

The old man scratched himself. "Haven't you ever been happy?" he demanded, with disapproval.

"Happy? Yes, sometimes. But in all my — expiations, there's never been a reconciliation. And what less," asked Heriot, "what less could I hope for?" (178–79)

The abstractness of this sort of reasoning brings about a distance between Heriot and the reader that creates a problem of credibility.

The largest gap in Stow's motivation of Heriot is in his movement of Heriot from hate and bitterness to love. For several scenes it seems as though the change will be brought about in a sort of Ancient Mariner recognition as Heriot comes to see the beauty in living creatures: the markings of a crocodile, the flight of ducks and geese, the fur of a wallaby. Heriot begs Justin to stop killing, even though he does so for food. Yet the final insight Heriot achieves is a vague one. He says, "God, what malice must have gone into creating a world where people have to eat. I renounce it" (167). He says further, "The earth hates us.... It heaves and strains under our feet." And, he continues to Justin, "The world wants us to prey. But I won't prey on you, no, I'll go against the world. Soon I won't prey on anything. Not even the insects this horse crushes carrying me." And further, "And hunger? Oh, God. Suppose you had an open wound. The maggots would be in it now, eating you up. That's hunger" (196).

The view Heriot holds of the foundation of the world certainly does not suggest a loving creator or a universal love underlying all creation, nor does it suggest that the bitterness has been driven from Heriot. Furthermore, Heriot does not at this point stop eating meat. Thus, when we get to Heriot's climactic speech to Justin concerning hate and love, the speech seems to come from the pen of the author, rather than through the regenerated mind of Heriot. Heriot says to Justin: "'I'm not so small as I was. No, I'm growing now. There are powers in me. I have love, and courage, a little of it, and reason of a sort, and compassion. And I'm a very beautiful machine, Justin, and so are you, although we're so fragile'" (196). And concerning Rex, Heriot says:

"I want them to know I didn't hate him. I didn't, Justin. It was because I loved him — loved all your people — that I did — that thing I did. They'll understand that. They'll know there never was one of them I hated. They'll remember, some of them, loving a woman and finding she was no good and wanting to kill her. And if they realize then it was love, not hate, that drove them, they'll understand me and forgive me. Tell them that."

"I'll tell them," Justin said softly.

"It's my only defence. It's the world's only defence, that we hurt out of love, not out of hate." (192–93)

And thus we are at the conclusion of the journey and the novel. And supposedly we have come with Heriot through his passion and his despair into peace. And yet, because the motivation has not been effectively presented, nor Heriot's changes clearly delineated, the conclusion of the novel and its ultimate meaning are in themselves vague.

First, there is the time Heriot spends alone in the cave with the pile of bones and rock paintings:

Long afterwards he got to his feet again and walked towards the mouth of the cave close by the pond. And under hanging rock he saw the first of the paintings, the crude figure of a man without a mouth, his head outlined with a horseshoe shape like that of the rainbow serpent.

"I know you," he said. "You are Wolaro. God. What does it matter what you're called."

He called to Justin: "Look, here is god." (193)

Justin is afraid, but he moves into the cave with Heriot. Stow writes of Heriot: "He was very tired. He lay down against the cave wall and closed his eyes, quiet and cool. 'I have come home now,' he said. 'This is home'" (39). What does this mean: "...here is god," or "I have come home now. This is home"? The only God we have been shown is the God who founded the world on prey and death. How can Heriot find home and comfort in the represented presence of such a God?

IV   *Theme*

Because it is difficult to follow Heriot's spiritual journey, to understand finally what he has learned, it is equally difficult to assess, with any certainty, Stow's intended meaning in the novel. Geoffrey Dutton sees the theme of *To the Islands* as a continuation of the search for permanence motif that Stow has dealt with in *A Haunted Land* and *The Bystander*.[11]

Although there are points in the novel to support Dutton's thesis, Heriot's comments on love, his shattering of the crucifix as an illustration of the impermanence of anything man can and does touch, the movement toward death, the expansion of these points to the fullness of an overriding theme in the novel is to give them a greater significance than they will bear. While Heriot initially sees himself and his life's work as coming to nothing, and wants to leave the mission because of this view, once he stones Rex and begins the journey through the wilderness there is no concern on his part with a need to make anything permanent or to find permanence. To prove this to be true, one need only look at those scenes I have just dealt with, the points at which Stow relates, however unsuccess-fully, Heriot's motivation. Dutton is on more stable ground as he suggests a comparison between Heriot and Andrew Maguire as men given to vanity and pride.

If one can see Heriot's journey as a movement from vanity to humility, as, like Dutton, T. Inglis Moore does,[12] a theme Patrick White illustrates in *Voss*, then the allegorical significance that Heriot and his journey are meant to suggest is a possibility. Yet, while there is some evidence that Heriot changes from the man who smashes the crucifix, as one who can bring down the world, to the man who realizes the helplessness of all living things, his own vulnerability and his own nothingness, the final scenes of the novel give little conclusive support to this change as the ultimate meaning of the novel.

Heriot's last concerns are several. He wants Justin to repeat his name from time to time to insure a certain degree of immortality. He makes the statement concerning love:

> "It's my only defence. It's the world's only defence, that we hurt out of love, not out of hate."
> "Yes, brother."
> "It's a feeble defence," said Heriot, with sadness, "and a poor reconciliation. But we've nothing better."(198)

These two points taken together, a concern with being remembered and a judgment on the universal nature of things, do not suggest a final extinction of self, or a depth of humility. Furthermore, Heriot's last act is one of assertion. Climbing to his final position as he looks out toward where the islands should be, Heriot takes up a block of stone fallen from the cliff.

> He knew suddenly the momentousness of his strength, his power to alter the world at will, to give the sea what the sea through an eternity of destruction was working to engulf, this broken rock. Truly, he would work a change on the world before it blinded him.
> Poised on the ledge, he threw the stone, and it floated slowly, slowly down the huge cliff face, and crashed against it. . . . (203)

Heriot's final statement, "My soul is a strange country," is the final ambiguity of the novel. If he has found peace, release through humility, why the adjective *strange,* why not a word of more definite meaning? Since there is no obvious correspondent coming before the last sentence to indicate the nature of *strange,* then the allegorical significance of the character of Heriot is in the conclusion of the novel as unclear as is the word *strange.* How can the reader participate in the allegory if the pattern is not filled in with enough clarity or consistency that he know what it is? In attempting to deal with the theme of the novel, then, one is in the same situation in which he finds himself in attempting to deal with Heriot's characterization and his motivation. Vincent Buckley sums up the problem succinctly when he writes that Heriot is "far too vague to bear the mythopoetic weight Stow puts on him."[13]

As a unified work of art, *To the Islands* must stand or fall through the characterization of Heriot; it is obvious that I think it falls. Yet, although the novel is uneven, Stow does some things quite well. As in the first two novels, his attention to detail in his evocation of place is excellent. His land is one of light and space and color, yet close up it is also a land of loneliness, of cyclone and darkness, of leprosy and trachoma. Furthermore, although Stow's minor white characters are no more than adequately drawn, without much to distinguish them, his rendering of the aborigines, with close attention to dialect and individuality, is excellent. Consider two passages. In the first Heriot is watching from the door of his hut; in the second he is ministering to an old woman he comes upon in an encampment in the outback.

...he watched Mabel walking through the grass. Djimbulangari slowly following. They moved like he did, loosely and tiredly, two old women with their hair tied in kerchiefs, their dresses hanging straight on their thin bodies. Looking at Mabel he thought that he had never seen her in any clothes but these, the dirty coloured skirt sewn to a flourbag bodice on which the mill brand was still bright green and legible. Picking their way like cranes through the grass, talking occasionally, not looking at one another. Old, dried-out women, useless and unwanted. (12)

He realized then that she was blind, and was filled with penitence, and went back to his camp under the rock where the foodbag was, and with his knife hacked open one of the precious tins. And he took it back to her and pushed pieces into her loose mouth. At first she struggled weakly to keep him away and turned her head from him, though she still kept her dog in order with one skinny hand. But then she tasted meat, and swallowed it, and turned to him with a grin that disclosed her great gums and the worn-down remnants of teeth just showing through them. He fed her until she was satisfied, and then she reached out and touched his shoulder with her hand, and leaned over and rested her forehead there. In that way they sat for what seemed a long time in that timeless place, naked brown woman by naked white man, and he stroked the loose skin of her back with tenderness, wanting to laugh, wanting to weep. (125)

It is the quality of writing in passages such as these that no doubt caused the early critics who gave *To the Islands* its two awards to overlook the problems in structure and characterization, and the problems brought about by the unsuccessful integration of realism and symbolism. The problems are real ones for Stow, however, and they are problems he faces again in *Tourmaline,* the novel that follows this one.

CHAPTER 5

Tourmaline

Tourmaline (1963) is Stow's most intriguing novel. It exhibits a greater imaginative power than his other books, and although not without some stylistic flaws, it shows Stow to be a writer in greater control of his material than he showed himself to be in *To the Islands*. As in *To the Islands*, in *Tourmaline* Stow is expanding his story by means of symbol and myth, but in *Tourmaline* the blending of the realistic and the mythic is more successful than in the former novel. In terms of language, Stow achieves a greater consistency than in the previous novels. Gone are the frequent quotations and literary allusions, and although there are a few instances of shifts into elevated diction, because of their position in the novel and the voice through which they are recorded, these shifts are not as jarring as similar ones in *To the Islands*. Perhaps a major reason for the greater consistency in language in *Tourmaline* is a restriction of point of view to that of a narrator-participant. The use of the Conradian type narrator is perfectly suited to the story Stow is telling, and by eliminating the possibility for omniscient pontificating, Stow has solved a basic problem in *To the Islands*.

Although there is some critical disagreement concerning Stow's characterization, a point that will be examined later, there is no fumbling toward credibility on Stow's part as with his characterization of Heriot. The most significant problems in *Tourmaline,* problems that are repetitions of similar problems in *To the Islands,* are those involving the theme, and the combining of symbols which suggest the theme and those involving the integration and illustration of philosophic thought and correspondent character action. Before considering at length narration, characterization, and the problems of working toward a meaning in *Tourmaline,* let me first reconstruct Stow's story, putting aside for the time being the symbolic or mythic implications that arise from it.

I *Plot*

As in all of Stow's novels, the sense of the particularity of place is important. All the novels are set in Western Australia, but in each of them one finds the characters conditioned not only by the land itself but further by their relation to their particular spatial limits: Malin, Koolabye, Strathmore, and Lingarin; the mission; Tourmaline; and Geraldton. A concern with the land, its freedoms, its demands, its limitations is perhaps the most consistent feature of Australian literature, and in this respect Stow's work is no exception. Whether Stow's concern with the effect of place on personality is in part brought about by his overview of the human predicament in terms of philosophic naturalism is a consideration I wish to hold in abeyance until I come to a final consideration of all the novels. At this point, I simply call the reader's attention to Stow's concern, for in *Tourmaline,* even more than in the other novels, the specifics of the setting on both the realistic and the symbolic level are of significance.

Tourmaline is a nearly deserted mining town, an isolated settlement at the dead end of a desert road. It is a place of red sun, shifting red dust, wind, crumbling buildings of stone and corrugated iron.

There is no stretch of land on earth more ancient than this. And so it is blunt and red and barren, littered with the fragments of broken mountains, flat, waterless.

. . .

At times, in the early morning, you would call this a gentle country. The new light softens it, tones flow a little, away from the stark forms. It is at dawn that the sons of Tourmaline feel for their heritage. Grey of dead wood, grey-green of leaves, set off a soil bright and tender, the tint of blood in water.

. . .

It is not the same country at five in the afternoon. That is the hardest time, when all the heat of the day rises, and every pebble glares, wounding the eyes, shortening the breath; the time when the practice of living is hardest to defend, and nothing seems easier than to cease, to become a stone, hot and still. At five in the afternoon there is one colour only, and that is brick-red, burning. After sunset, the blue dusk, and later the stars. The sky is the garden of Tourmaline.[1]

In the town itself there is Kestrel's Tourmaline Hotel "...of stone and rough plaster, once whitewashed, but now reddened with dust. The roofing iron is also of red, and advertizes a brand of beer no longer brewed. A verandah sheds the bare dirt on three sides" (8). There are Tom Spring's store and the jail, the only other important structures in Tourmaline. The narrator says:

Following the raw red streak of the road are the houses of Tourmaline: uniform, dilapidated, stained with the red dust. There are not many. At last, and apart, is a cube of stone, marked by a wooden sign as the police station. And behind it rises a fortress, a squat square tower open to the sky. This is my tower and prison; for I am the Law of Tourmaline.

On two stony hills to the north of the town stand the toppling masts of the mine and the hulk of the abandoned church. The church is of tender brown and rose stone. Beside it, an oleander impossibly persists in flowering. Planks are falling from the wooden bell-tower, but the bell is there still; and in dust-storms and on nights of high wind its irregular tolling sweeps away over Tourmaline to the south.

. . .

It is not a ghost town. It simply lies in a coma. This may never end. (8)

Once the wireless brought the outside world into Tourmaline, but now it is silent. Were it not for a supply truck that comes mysteriously once a month to Tourmaline, leaves a few items, and immediately returns to the outside world, Tourmaline would be in complete isolation.

Few people still live in Tourmaline: a handful of natives who live in the "camp," a couple of prospectors who live beyond the limit of the town, characters with names like Horse, Dicko, Bill the Dill, Agnes Day (Agnus Dei); those important to the story are Kestrel, the hotel owner, barkeeper, a man of pride, selfishness and an uneasy nature, given to hatred and contempt for those around him; Deborah, the half-caste mistress of Kestrel; Byrne, nephew of Kestrel, the young town drunk and half-wise fool; Tom Spring, the objective, clear-seeing storekeeper of Tourmaline and his wife Mary; the narrator who is known as The Law of Tourmaline.

The narrator catches the people of Tourmaline in a photographic still: "Outside, under Kestrel's verandah, men sat in the dust; propped against a wall, sharp knees drawn up, with glasses in their hands. Ah, Tourmaline is a great leveller. Their clothes, their bark faces, their attitudes were identical; their lassitude was a communal affair, or perhaps a form of pestilence" (12). The scene is suddenly changed with the announcement of a truck: "All of us, all Tourmaline, gathered in the street. And the truck slowly coming, its hot green paint powdered with Tourmaline dust, a grotesque hand of yellow metal dangling beside the driver's door. Waiting, all of us" (13).

The truck this day brings someone new to Tourmaline, the first new man in many years, for the town has ceased to exist for those beyond it. The man, Michael Random, is young, still in his twenties, blond, but on this day near death from long exposure in the desert sun. Dumped at Kestrel's hotel, Michael, eyes swollen and closed, the pulse almost gone, is seen immediately as "a new life for Tourmaline."

Mary Spring, Deborah, Byrne, The Law — all take turns nursing the stranger until the danger is passed. When he can speak, he answers their questioning of his identity with, "Up to you." He tells them that he has come "from the other end of the road," that during his pain he has thought himself to be "in hell," and that "wild beasts are loose in the world." He finally tells them, "I am a diviner." The narrator, The Law, standing by, says, "What a bound of my heart there was to think that it was this we had saved for Tourmaline. A diviner in our midst, in our waterless and dying town" (26).

A diviner by talent, by occupation, Michael gradually becomes the symbol of the Divine for most of Tourmaline. Like Ahab's doubloon, the diviner seems for the people of Tourmaline to represent what each most wants. In the beginning many look to him as a possibility for new hope, some as a hope for more gold for Tourmaline, but others see him more importantly as a source to bring more water, water to make the desert town live again. For Deborah he is a man of imagination who has "done something," who has been beyond the confines of Tourmaline. She sees him not only as a spark of spiritual fire, but as a sexual power, and she wants him to give her a son. For the narrator, who observes and records the past and present of Tourmaline, Michael comes to represent a possibility of spiritual rebirth, as the hope that will further the "espirit de corps,'' as he frequently refers to the bond of the people of Tourmaline. Two men in the town resist the lure of Michael: Kestrel, for whom Michael represents a threat as the people turn from him and his quasi-leadership to follow Michael; and Tom Spring, who sees through Michael and identifies him as one of those "wild beasts" let loose in the world.

Michael sees himself and his relationship to the town ambivalently: in part as the result of a continuing delusion that God persecutes him, in part through the initial regard and expectation that the town has of him. He is like Flannery O'Conner's Hazel Moates; he is "God-crazed," and like him he is in no way gentle or Christlike. Early, while bathing his burned body, Mary, Deborah, and others see a hollow scar over his left breast and another "on the back opposite." What he does not tell them is that the scars are from a previous suicide attempt, and it is not until later that they learn that his coming to Tourmaline was not intentional, but another miscarried suicide attempt. As Michael recognizes the expectation the town has of him, he comes to believe in his power, concluding that God saved him in the wilderness so that he might save Tourmaline. To old Gloria, the only one who has continued to take care of the ruined church, he asks,

"Do you believe I've found God?"
"I dunno," she said, "How you tell?"
"Through pain," he said. . . . "Shame, weakness. He makes me suffer. Persecutes me. Won't let me go. So I know I've found him." (77)

The weeks pass. Michael moves alone to an abandoned hut on the edge of town. With a newly fashioned divining rod he discovers a reef of gold. Although the town does not really need gold, having the meager sufficiency it requires, the discovery of gold by Michael is to them a sign of his power, and his following increases.

Kestrel, however, is not one of the converts. Rejected by Deborah and bored with himself and his role in Tourmaline, still convinced of the diviner's quackery, Kestrel decides to leave Tourmaline. This is an incredible decision as the townspeople see it, for no one in recent memory has left Tourmaline and been able to return. Nevertheless, Kestrel gathers his gold and throws open his bar to the people of Tourmaline the night before his departure. The drunken brawl he has no doubt hoped for occurs, and order is restored not by Kestrel or The Law but by Michael, as he now assumes the leadership of Tourmaline. When later The Law asks the diviner his business, he answers, "To speak for God," ... "Because he spoke to me, in the wilderness. Now I'm his mouthpiece" (78).

With a sense of his importance and his mission, Michael proceeds to revive the now eager Tourmaline. Building a bonfire on the hill near the church and having one of the natives ring the church bell, he dramatically calls the startled people out into the clear night and up the hillside to the church. In a trancelike state Tourmaline pours into the church and in a kind of rapture begins to sing. The Law says:

> I looked down, from the height of the stars, and saw us united. All Tourmaline, all together; elbow by elbow, cheek by jowl, singing as one, shouting and weeping as one, praising God, beseeching God, wordless, passionate. I felt the power of our unity rise towards the stars like waves of heat from hot rock. (136–37)

With the bell tolling, the guitar, the singing and the moaning, and with the diviner speaking to them, the ecstasy continues: 'He Mongga!' Charlie cried out, from the altar. And from everywhere murmurs and shouts came. 'Mongga! Mongga!' And an old strained voice in tears said: 'He is Christ.' These vaguely familiar tones I recognized (oh God) as mine" (138).

A few days after this night, Tourmaline is awakened at dawn to follow Michael across the dry bed of the Tourmaline lake, for he feels the time has come for him to divine for water, to test God and himself, and to bring about the rebirth that Tourmaline has been awaiting. The diviner chooses his spot and instructs the men to dig one hundred and fifty feet. Days pass. The measurement is reached, exceeded. Nothing.

> He turned away, raising his hands to his eyes. And he cried out, in a voice that didn't seem to be the voice of anyone we knew: "It was there! The water was there. God's betrayed me."
> One last flicker of his flame before it died. Then all was over. He was nothing. (163)

After the defeat, The Law writes, "Life goes on; as I have often, in my long life, had cause to remind myself. One sleeps and feeds.

And, once a month, the truck comes." The truck does come and
with it Kestrel.

> When the truck stopped, Kestrel got out and went to his front door and
> opened it. And he stood there, holding it open, while three men climbed
> out from beneath the tarpaulin and went past him into the hotel. They
> walked quickly, not looking round. But I was apart from the others, and
> caught a glimpse of one of them. He had no nose or mouth; only teeth. I
> tried to pray for him. And for us. (164)

One order has passed away, and a new one is beginning. Just
what the new Kestrel with his new organizing principle will be,
Tourmaline is not sure.

> The breeze hissed across country. The sun went down. No bell, No fire.
> The diviner kept to his hut, up there on the black hillside.
> The strangers were shut up in the hotel, seen by no one.
> At the mine Jack Speed lay alone in his tall room.
> In the shack behind the garden Rock washed his shirt, in dishwater.
> Tom's cat, on the step of the store, slapped the face of Kestrel's dog and
> fled.
> While the people at the camp mourned; keening. Raising their eyes to
> the cold white stars, that promise nothing. (167)

Kestrel sets about drawing Tourmaline to him: Deborah, Byrne,
Mary, but not Tom Spring. Just as he has refused to give himself to
the diviner, he now refuses to give his support to Kestrel, but
Kestrel soon has the town as he wants it; and at his store counter
one day, Tom Spring dies.

Michael appears a final time, and is spotted by Byrne as he is
leaving Tourmaline. In a confession of love, Byrne, the hopeless
Byrne, begs the diviner, "Stay here."

> "What," said the diviner, "to be equal with you? God forbid."
> And he went away, towards the leaning fence that marks the end of the
> road. Dust blew back from where his thick boots fell.
> "Mike," Byrne called. He dropped his guitar and went after him.
> But the diviner broke into a spring, and leaped the trailing barbed wire
> of the fence, and ran away laughing, into the gathering wind. (170)

The narrator, his friend dead, leaves Tom Spring's store and walks out into the blowing dust. His record of Tourmaline ends with speculation:

And the bell, up on the hill, kept tolling. Purposeless; moved by the wind.

There was no town, no hill, no landscape. There was nothing. Only myself, swimming through the red flood, that had covered the world and spared me only, of all of those who had been there.

Dust lay over the chimneys of Lacey's Find; over the lone billiard table in the desert. It silted up the stock route well at Dave Speed's camp. It heaped in the sockets of the diviner's eyes.

Wild beasts were loose on the world. Terrors would come. But wonders, too, as in the past. Terrors and wonders, as always.

. . .

The bell tolled. The thick wind whirled. Caught in the current, drowning, I ceased to struggle, and let it bear me up the road. There was no town, no landscape. What could this be if not the end of the world?

Then the wind dropped for half a minute. And I saw my tower, the boundary of Tourmaline, waiting. (174)

II *"The Law" and Other Characters*

This outline does an injustice to the novel, for the power of *Tourmaline* lies not in the plot but in Stow's excellent creation of the sense of place, of drama and impending drama, of the interplay of need and possibility. Stow's success along these lines is in large part due to his choice of a narrator-participant to tell his story. He chooses from among his town's people an old man known as The Law. Something of a Tiresias, yet without the power to see clearly beyond the present, The Law sees in himself the function of recorder; he is old, he tells us, and because of this he can remember Tourmaline as it once was when the mine was operating, when there was water and prosperity, when the dead pepper trees which line the street of Tourmaline were alive. His home, his "cell," the gaol, and gaol yard are strewn with old letters and papers blown by the wind, records of voices and struggles long ago ceased. His mind is filled with images of the serenity of his lost youth, a time of "easter lilies in our old garden; the smooth, pink lilies, so tough, so delicate that sprang up leafless from the baked ground"; images of change and waste, of the once neighboring Lacey's Find, now buried in the blowing red dust, of the present "coma" of Tourmaline. Registering through his years the understanding of the transitory state of manmade things and man himself, The Law, though old and tired, has little of Heriot's world-weariness. He has still the possibility of hope, a certain childlike curiosity, an idealistic nature that overcomes his reason and sweeps him into the diviner craze with most of the rest of Tourmaline. He has that peculiar divided state of consciousness that allows him to observe, participate, and observe himself participating. As much a character as any one else in the novel, the narrator can and does change. He is mistaken and confused, and sometimes his perceptions are not trustworthy. It is this humanness that makes him an excellent lens through which to filter the life of Tourmaline.

As I have said, Stow gives the novel from the beginning to The Law. The story is the record The Law has preserved, is preserving, of what happened in that seasonless time when Tourmaline was visited by a diviner, spiritually awakened, and then abandoned — changed and confused — to a different kind of force represented by the newly determined Kestrel. It is this period in Tourmaline's history and the narrator's memory that he wishes to describe. Since the story is the important thing, he develops the cast in his drama only so much as their individual characters are beneficial to the events in his story. He is not omniscient. He writes at the beginning of his story, "There is much I must invent, much I have not seen. Guesses, hints, like pockets of dust in the crevices of conversation." (10) There is a certain dreamlike quality about Tourmaline, as realistic or as free floating as the narrator's imagination at any one point re-creates it. He brings a chracter out of the dust of his memory, places him before the reader like a motion picture still, and once his image is familiar to the reader, the reel begins to turn and the stills flow together as the story is set in motion.

The introduction of Tom and Mary Spring illustrates the narrator's method:

To begin, I must imagine and invent.

Tom Spring, on a rickety chair, behind the counter of his store, sleeves rolled up on his thin strong arms. A small strong thin man, Tom; quiet, so quiet one might stop and listen, in surprise. A deep Quaker quiet, an act of religion, that might help his soul to become like a great cave and trap and amplify the faint whisperings of God — that was the silence he was building, behind his quiet eyes, under his thinning hair. Imagine him there.

And Mary, in the kitchen perhaps, or coming in to spray the flies (which, it could be, she heard from another room, shattering the holy calm), with her dark greying hair and her plump arms, her immovable charity. Imagine her there. (12)

Leonie Kramer is wrong when she criticizes *Tourmaline* because, as she says, "...character is generalized to the point of extinction."[2] While it is true that Stow's intention through his choice of narrator and his narrator's limitations is not to deal at length with any one of Tourmaline's people, but rather to deal with them collectively in their contact with and reaction to the diviner, it is not true that they are bodiless figures, manipulated as symbols to illustrate a particular theme. On the contrary, it is to Stow's credit that within the given design of the novel, characters are individualized to the degree that they are.

Among the major characters there are several that are particularly well done. There is Byrne, the drunken, ballad-making, emotional cripple of Tourmaline. A figure seemingly evolved through Tommy Cross in *A Haunted Land* and Keithy Farnham in *The Bystander,* dependent like them, yet wise in his understanding of himself and his needs, he gives voice to the mood of Tourmaline as he sings his mournful ballads.

Deborah and Michael, though their individual characters are not explored at length, emerge more credibly in their dramatic scenes than do any other of Stow's would-be lovers. Perhaps it is because Stow is expressing hostility rather than tenderness, but regardless of the reason, gone is the wooden dialogue, the fumbling for expression:

"What are you?" he demanded, frozen and trembling. "A harlot?"
As it happened that was a word she knew. And she cried to him: "No, no, I'm not. I'm honest. I love you." She was humble and defiant, brilliant and sombre.
"Ah," he said, "you're like an animal, you hot bitch. Go home to your husband."
"He's not my husband."
"Of course he is, in the sight of God."
"What do you know about the sight of God?"
"More than you think, maybe."
She tossed her head, a wild meaningless gesture. She was trying not to

cry, perhaps. "I can't love him. He won't let me. You know him, you can believe that, can't you?"

"So you thought you'd come to me?"

She said, quite simply: "I want to have your baby." (90)

Michael, for all that goes unexplained about him — and we are not given enough clues to speculate beyond what the narrator knows and reveals of him — is a far more convincing character than is his God-driven predecessor in *To the Islands*. His interior state is revealed dramatically in a way that Heriot's never is. The level of his diction is never inconsistent, nor does it sound stilted as does Heriot's. In his attack on Deborah in the previous quotation, in his callous rejection of Byrne's admiration, in his self-hatred and cruelty, his voice gives insight into a distinct personality, rather than one wandering into vagueness as Heriot's rhetorical outbursts suggest.

The character of the narrator, though drawn incompletely and indirectly, is also, given Stow's objective, clearly drawn. Never the focal point of the novel, the narrator emerges at the end as the character with whom the reader shares the greatest intimacy and the greatest understanding.

Even the minor characters spring to life. Stow succeeds with his cynical prospector Dave Speed and with old Gloria, the "self-appointed vergeress" of the dilapidated church, much as he succeeded with Nakala and Fred in *The Bystander*.

Leonie Kramer complains that the characters' growth in *Tourmaline* is "stunted by the necessity for all to conform to the myth."[3] Again, Kramer mistakes the kind of novel Stow is writing. The characters do change in the course of their encounter with Michael, and in this change is the possibility for growth. Even Michael himself changes. No one is quite the same at the end of the novel as he was in the beginning. Yet, Stow does not deal with growth as such, for he is far more interested in the phenomenon of the diviner and the total experience surrounding him than in an extended study of any one of the characters. *To the Islands* is an extended study of character and Heriot demands development; on the other hand, because of Stow's concern in *Tourmaline,* no character requires any more extensive treatment or "growth" than Stow gives him. It is not a question of a character's conforming to the myth, but rather a question of the proportion of development that the plan of the novel requires.

III *Place as Symbol*

The problems that do arise in *Tourmaline,* and these are problems that detract from rather than seriously impair the novel, come with an attempt to understand Stow's meaning in the novel, to put all the allusions and symbols together and to interpret the novel on the symbolic and mythic level. To illustrate this problem, let us first look at some of the questions that are raised and some of the allusions that are suggested.

There is the town itself. We are asked to see it as both real and symbolic. On the symbolic level there is no problem. Blowing red dust, hard baked earth, dead pepper trees, no rain and little water, virtual sterility, a single church and it in ruins, its bell tolling aimlessly in the wind; the people moving in a comatose state, waiting. Its leader, Kestrel, nervous and purposeless, impotent to act. Isolated, dying, desolate, Tourmaline (its name a carryover from Malin in *A Haunted Land*?) is Stow's Waste Land — Fisher King, ruined chapel, red rock, sterility — all the appointments are there, except the rain.

On the realistic level one questions the existence of Tourmaline in its relation to the outside world, questions, indeed, the existence of the outside world itself. We are told that Tourmaline is sustained by the monthly deliveries of a single truck:

Perhaps it was natural that we should be in awe of him, the driver of the truck. After all, it was many years that he had been coming, once a month, from the back of the blue ranges; and always he hugged to himself the mystery of his life's true ambience, as if it could endanger us. He would hardly speak. He was as zealous as a grandmother guarding the facts of life. (14)

Why does the truck come to Tourmaline? Why do not others come? What is the meaning of the truck driver and his secrecy? Why does no one leave Tourmaline, and when Kestrel does, how has he been changed and what are the men he brings back? How do the people of Tourmaline live? There is some water, but what is its source? And the outside world — the narrator says: "But when I am quiet and alone, and have turned on the wireless (as on every morning for — ah, too many years) and have spoken, and have listened, and as on every morning since these terrible times began have heard no answer'' (9). When the diviner starts to tell of the outside world, the narrator interrupts him:

> "You mustn't tell us," I said suddenly. Because I was afraid. Because of the danger — the terrible danger. It was as if my silent wireless had finally spoken, and for Tourmaline's sake I must clap my hands to my ears, and close my mind, and hear nothing — nothing — but the gathering wind, perhaps, and the slow soft hush of sand at every door. (37)

Why can't the reader learn something of the outside world and more about Tourmaline? The questions are ones that tease the imagination, but at the same time leave the reader with a nagging feeling that Stow does not have the answers himself.

A. D. Hope, in "Randolph Stow and the Tourmaline Affair," dismisses these problems and those Kramer raises about character with the statement, ". . . Tourmaline is not a real world at all and makes no pretence of it. It is a science-fiction sort of situation."[4] Certainly, Tourmaline has some of the attributes of science fiction, but it is not, finally, science fiction; and because it is not, one cannot avoid the feeling that on the realistic level Stow might have built his structure with a little more firmness.

IV *Characters as Symbol; Theme of* Tourmaline

When we attempt to understand the meaning of the characters in terms of what Stow intends them to represent, there are additional complications. The complications and the confusion come from Stow's weighting the story with details suggestive of the Christian myth, details that make it unclear, at least in the beginning of the novel, whether the reader is to interpret the characters allegorically or whether the Christian coloring is merely incidental. For example, the names: Mary, Deborah, Michael, Agnes Day, Tom Spring. One searches in vain for a specific correspondence. Is Tom Spring meant to suggest a "doubting Thomas," or a spring of truth, or a rebirth? What is the significance of the narrator's remembering Easter lilies? And why is a rooster crowing in Mary's yard the afternoon the nearly dead diviner is brought into Tourmaline? Even the angelic description of the diviner and the birth imagery surrounding his arrival are further attempts to play upon the reader's suggestability. And given these suggestions, the reader is prepared to see the unfolding of the story in terms of allegory, until it becomes apparent that the choice of names, the Christian allusions, are not important to the story that the narrator is telling. Stow, I suppose, wanted to charge the atmosphere with hints of the Christian myth in order to intensify the parallel he is making, but he does the reader a disservice by giving him a false start. It is only when the reader is able to distance himself from the narrator and the townspeople and see their delusion as they interpret the diviner as a savior — when a native cries "He Mongga!" and the narrator cries "He is Christ!" — that the reader understands what the true nature of the story is. It is not a reenactment of the Christian myth in the sense that Stow intends the reader to interpret the diviner as a savior or as the returned Christ, but rather the emphasis is on the town's mistaken view of the diviner in terms of the awaited Redeemer.

The mythic design that overrides the entire novel projects Tourmaline as a microcosm of the world as it waits for rebirth, regeneration, be it in terms of a positive or a negative force. "Beware of false prophets," Stow's story illustrates, and beware of an incautious interpretation of things contemporary in terms of the old, the accepted myths.

In addition to the general problems in interpretation, there are numerous problems in the interpretation of the focal character, Michael. What does it mean that he has enough talent to divine gold, but not water? Does he have the power and it leaves him, as he says, or can he only continue the sterility that has come upon Tourmaline? Though these questions go unanswered, the overall significance of Michael the deluder and the self-deluded is clear enough.

The most vague of the major characters in *Tourmaline* is Kestrel. There are numerous scenes in which Kestrel reveals himself; for example, in conversation with the narrator: "'I might be the sanest bloke in Tourmaline, I wouldn't be surprised, but I have my days of wanting to run amok. I can't breathe here. I want to bash the walls down and get some air. What the hell is there for a man like me to do? Is this all the life there is?'" (102).

The name Kestrel means "falcon" — a bird of prey — and there are examples of Kestrel's cruelty, his "preying" on Byrne and

Deborah; and yet just exactly what Stow means for Kestrel to represent is unclear. The narrator says of him:

And as I listened to him I began to have a good deal of pity for him, because he was the man he was, trapped in his selfhood as the flies in the bar were trapped in their small cages; but also I began to fear him, I began to hate him, and I could not explain to myself why.... I was afraid of him, and I could not meet his eyes, which were so unusually honest. (108)

And Tom Spring, whose voice it seems we are to accept as authority, says, "They're two sides of a coin," ... "Shadows of one another" (147).

We are told these things about Kestrel, and if he is truly a dark force in the novel, if we are to see him as another false prophet or demonic counter of or counterpart to Michael, then quite a bit more development is called for. As with the questions that remain about the reality of Tourmaline, the ambiguity of Kestrel is not so much an intriguing one as it is an ambiguity that brings about the uncomfortable suspicion that Stow has not worked out the meaning of Kestrel in his own mind. In spite of wild beast allusions in connection with Kestrel, the allusion of the name itself, and the echo of Yeats' "The Second Coming" with the implication that Kestrel and his Fedallahlike henchmen will be the new organizing principle around which Tourmaline will form itself, there is no specific indication that Kestrel with his new knowledge of the outside world will be an evil force in Tourmaline. Perhaps Stow means only to indicate that Kestrel's power will be nonspiritual in nature and therefore negative; and yet if the only spiritual alternative is represented by the suicidal diviner, then both choices seem poor ones; and though perhaps this is ultimately the meaning of the novel, the problem remains that the symbolic function of Kestrel is not made clear.

The gulf between the philosophic assertions that the characters make as to the meaning of the events in Tourmaline and the action on which these assertions are based is not as wide in *Tourmaline* as it is in *To the Islands*. And yet, perhaps the meaning in the novel would be clearer if no assertions were made, if the reader were left to interpret the diviner phenomenon on his own. The problem that arises comes from not knowing which character in the novel to listen to, or how much to accept from any one character. Since the reader has been viewing the story through the eyes of the narrator, his first inclination is to accept The Law's pronouncement on the events as synonymous with Stow's own views. For example, the narrator philosophizing on the nature of man remarks, "It came to me suddenly that a man is a disease of God, and that God must surely die." He follows this by relating a French fairy tale:

> There was a well beneath a great tree. And in the tree was a princess, in hiding. And by the well, a hideous, pathetic, ludicrous negress, with a pitcher on her shoulder.
> The negress was gazing into the well; which reflected not her, but the face of the princess among the leaves. The black woman's vast teeth showed in delight.
> "Ah, *comme je suis belle!*" *s'écria la negresse.*
> A joke, then — was it?
> Oh you in the branches.
> I don't find that funny. (84)

What do these statements, juxtaposed as they are, mean? "Man is a disease of God," and the assumption that God deludes man into thinking himself beautiful. The events in the novel simply do not illustrate these ideas sufficiently. Man is not killing God; no one in the novel is shown to be truly evil. Through the diviner God may be playing a trick on man, but this seems only to be the diviner's interpretation. One man's delusion, brought about in part by a town's yearnings, does not justify such a metaphysical generalization. The problem is further complicated by one's not being able to discount the narrator's ideas entirely. To be able to accept what he believes as a thematic statement one must examine his ideas in light of the total story, to try to sift out what is right and wrong. Again this seems an unnecessary burden on the reader, but this is Stow's method. For example, The Law says at the conclusion of the novel: "There is no sin but cruelty. Only one. And that original sin, that began when a man first cried to another, in his matted hair, Take charge of my life, I am close to breaking" (174). The consequences of this sin of wanting to put oneself into the hands of another and to make him responsible is illustrated through the story. Byrne has put himself in the hands of Kestrel and takes his physical and verbal abuse. He projects his own longings for a father to the diviner soon after Michael has been brought into Tourmaline. In reply to the narrator's statement, "Tourmaline seems to have taken charge of him [the diviner]. When he wakes up he's going to feel he's not his own property any more," Byrne remarks, "He mightn't want to be his own property. . . . Why would he?" (20). Byrne tries to give himself to the diviner. He is rejected. Deborah and the town try the same thing. The diviner tries to give himself, force himself on God. Apparently he is rejected. And finally Byrne, Deborah, Mary Spring, and most likely all of Tourmaline but Tom Spring give themselves to Kestrel. It is Tom Spring who has consistently rejected the idea of giving up the self to follow anyone. He has said no to both Michael and Kestrel, and because he illustrates both in action and in philosophical statement the rejection of this temptation to give oneself up, a temptation that proves to be the downfall of all who succumb, Tom Spring, through his restraint and his objectivity, seems to be the one character whose words most clearly illustrate Stow's intended meaning in the novel. It is he who identifies Michael and Kestrel as "two sides of a coin," seeing both of them as "wild beasts." The narrator has described Tom Spring in the beginning: "A deep Quaker quiet, an act of religion, that might help his soul to become like a great cave and trap and amplify the faint whisperings of God — that was the silence he was building. . ." (12).

In refusing to join the diviner, Tom Spring answers the diviner's question of "What's your belief?" with "I'm still waiting. . . . Who'd dare say before the end of the road." Tom continues, "We'll live till we die. . . . If we believe we exist, that's enough" (38). Before he dies he admonishes Kestrel to "Honor the single soul" (172). At one point Tom Spring is criticizing the narrator for giving himself so gullibly to the diviner, and he tries to explain his own views of God to him. The narrator writes:

He unveiled his God to me, and his God had names like the nameless, the sum of all, the ground of being. He spoke of the unity of opposites, and of the overwhelming power of inaction. He talked of becoming a stream, to carve out canyons without ceasing always to yield; of being a tree to grow without thinking; of being a rock to be shaped by winds and tides. He said I must become empty in order to be filled, must unlearn everything, must accept the role of fool. (148)

Tom Spring continues to explain his Taoistic beliefs to the uncomprehending narrator. His inability to make clear his beliefs stands for the complexity of man's relationship to the unknown. "To speak for God," as the diviner reveals his mission to be, is a foolish vanity, an impossibility. And those who would give themselves over to any power who would assume control of them or responsibility for them would deny the struggle toward self-realization that each man must take upon himself.

Although there are problems in *Tourmaline,* Stow's achievement in the novel is impressive. It is quite an original book, one that would assure Stow a place in the history of Australian literature had he written nothing else.

CHAPTER 6

The Merry-Go-Round in the Sea

WHEN Randolph Stow was twenty-nine he turned to impressions from his childhood and wrote quite a beautiful novel, *The Merry-Go-Round in the Sea*. He turned from his experiments in myth and symbol in *To the Islands* and *Tourmaline* to write a realistic narrative rich in poetry, poetry made of a child's impressionistic gathering unto himself of his bright seaside world in Western Australia. He allowed himself a freedom in *The Merry-Go-Round in the Sea* that was not possible in other novels structured according to the requirements of plot and the additional requirements of allegory or myth. Whereas in the earlier novels the attention to setting and its subsequent rendering was make subordinate, in *The Merry-Go-Round in the Sea* Stow is not so much telling a story as he is telling a place, a time; thus the descriptive power that the reader ahs come to appreciate in the earlier novels is given full expression in *The Merry-Go-Round in the Sea*.

Freedom from the strictures of plot is brought about by Stow's emphasis on character, specifically the character of Rob Coram as he grows in understanding and perception, passing through and beyond the years of World War II, in his own span of time from the age of six to the age of fourteen. As with Keithy Farnham in *The Bystander,* Stow moves with ease and delicacy into the mind of Rob Coram, and the lyric evocation of childhood is very much that of a specific child with a humor, an understanding, and a vision all his own, and yet, sensitive, inquisitive, a little uncertain and unaccepting of the changes in his expanding world. Rob Coram is Stow's Portrait of the Artist as a Young Australian.

There is little need for critical exploration in *The Merry-Go-Round in the Sea*. There are no philosophical points in question, no technical innovations, and the insights that come to and through Rob Coram produce more of a nod and a smile of recognition than a sense of profundity. While there are points for the critic to consider — specifically Stow's use of point of view, his focus in the second half of the novel, his use of the merry-go-round symbol, and the novel's structure — there are no serious problems. The critic who comes to *The Merry-Go-Round in the Sea* finds himself for the most part in the pleasant position of simply indicating what Stow does well. In view of this, I shall combine an introduction to the novel with critical comments as specific points arise in the progression of the novel, concluding with a critical summary based on the accumulation of observations.

I *Plot, Rob, and Point of View*

To summarize *The Merry-Go-Round in the Sea* in any succinct fashion is to do the novel an injustice, for there is the loosest of plots, and no progressive sampling of incidents will quite reveal the wealth of life it contains. The story is divided into two lengthy sections unified by the presence or absence of Rick Maplestead, cousin of the young protagonist Rob Coram. As the novel opens Rob is being taken by his mother to the Maplestead home to spend a last evening with Rick before he leaves for the war. All the children love the handsome young man, but Rob especially idolizes him, seeing him as he never sees his father or any other adult, as a model for his own being. A sampling of dialogue will reveal the nature of their relationship and Stow's method of presenting it:

The brush stopped moving, and Rick turned. "Hey," he said. "It's my young cousin. Coming to get his hair done." He reached out with the brush, and the boy ducked back, covering his hair with his hands.
"Don't," he said, laughing. "Don't Rick."
Rick leaned against Goldie and took off his hat. His brown hair was ridged by the hat and damp at the edges, and he rubbed at it with his wrist, still holding the brush. Rick's face was brown, which made his eyes look very white where they were white and very blue where they were blue. There was a little bit of gold in one of his teeth.
"Well," he said, "Where have you been?"
"Home," said the boy.
"You didn't come and see me. I had your swag laid out on the bed, and you didn't come."
"I've come now," said the boy.
"It's too late. You've hurt my feelings."

"Oh, bulldust," said the boy.

"Hey, who taught you to say that?"

"You did."

"Did I?" said Rick. "You ever heard me talk like that Goldie?"

"She has," Rob said. "She nodded."

"She's a lying bitch," said Rick.

The boy laughed and laughed, looking up at Rick's face, which he loved. "You shouldn't say that."

"Ah, but you won't tell, will you?"

"When I swear Grandma puts mustard on my tongue."

"Does she do that?" said Rick. "Your grandma's a fierce old lady."

The boy was breathless, he had the giggles. There was nothing on earth less fierce than his grandma. Rick's blue eyes were fixed on him with interest.

"If everyone thought I was as funny as you do," Rick said, "I could go on the pictures and make a million dollars."

"You're just goofy," said the boy. He looked at Rick's slow smile, and the little glint of gold.

. . .

Rick was walking to the gate, and Goldie was following. The boy looked down from the sky. He looked down on Rick holding open the gate, and closing it while Goldie waited. He looked down on Rick walking ahead in the road, being nudged now and then by Goldie's nose, but not turning. The hairs on the back of Rick's neck were golden. Two crows were crying in the sky, and everything was asleep. The day, the summer, would never end. He would walk behind Rick, he would study Rick forever.[1]

With Rick gone to war, time passes. Stow writes a phrase that he often repeats, "The boy's life had no progression, his days led nowhere." Stow continues, "He woke in the morning in his room and at night he slept: the wheel turning full circle, the merry-go-round of his life revolving" (44). The boy's world is a world of sensory impressions: the smell of yeast rising and bean flowers wilting and Aunt Molly teasing wool, the "ark-ark" of crows and the kangaroo dog he used to ride, "the smell of chaff and a taste of saltbush" (47).

The days are filled with adult events and adult words of the war: "Batavia," and "Surabaya." Refugees come into the town and then soldiers. Tennis courts are turned into trenches; air raid sirens break the quiet and the boy begins to learn there is something called death.

As soldiers move through Geraldton and the coastal town is

thought to be unsafe, the family moves inland, to Andarra. The whole world is a mystery to Rob and each change an event. Stow writes, "Now that the boy lived at Andarra, he lived in an enchanted place." He describes Andarra:

> The garden was a riot, a jungle, which could not be comprehended in its entirety. It was a tall palm tree rattling high in the sky above the gate. It was dark clumps of olives and oleander. It was a hedge of sour, clean-smelling citrons. It was a stone wall in a thicket of curtain-pole bamboo. It was Geraldton wax plant grown into trees, and flowering, where children could perch like birds and talk very seriously. And for the boy, it was above all the roses.
>
> The white roses had taken over one side of the veranda. They engulfed shrubs at the front of the house, and clothed the dead stump of an old palm. The fragile scent of them was everywhere, mixed with citrus and eucalyptus. The flowers, the dark neat leaves, became the boy's image of perfection. (73–74)

Months pass, and then one year and another. Relatives, poems, books, war talk, the land, school, boyish adventures, and from time to time a thought of Rick, a question of his whereabouts; but Rick is missing in action and Rob's questions are evaded.

Though the events that fill Rob's world are loosely structured, not even sequential enough to be called episodic, Stow is working with a plan in mind. One structural device that he uses to unify his material is a method of fading out one scene or chapter and fading in the one that follows, keeping the subject the same. His technique is particularly effective in the few switches from the security of Rob's childhood world to the prisoner of war camp where Rick is being held in Malaya and vice versa. One chapter set in the prison camp ends: "The tears flowed, dropping on the clasped hands on the floor. The tears would never stop. 'We're young,' he whispered, looking down at the normal hands. 'Hughie. We're young. We're young'" (96). The next chapter begins in the Australian school room.

> Donny Webb was reciting, singsong:
> They shall grow not old, as we that
>   are left grow old;
> Age shall not weary them, nor the
>   years condemn. . . . (97)

In the four years that Rick is away Rob grows both in ways that change a child into a boy, and in the kinds of awareness that Stow would suggest give rise to the emerging poet. Of the practical things, Rob learns of sex, that babies come to humans from doing things similar to what cows and bulls do. "Life, it seemed, was not at all as described in *Cole's Funny Picture Book,* and he felt bitterly about Mr. Cole, who must have been sniggering all the time behind his Burke-and-Wills beard" (139).

Rob learns about the war: "For the first time in his life he began to read the newspaper, poring over the dark photographs of Hiroshima and Nagasaki, of the bomb itself, and the mushroom cloud that had now taken root in the world like an upas tree" (146). And Rob learns about life outside Geraldton as he travels with his mother and sister for two weeks in Perth:

> The city smelled exotic, extraordinary. It smelled of fruit in the green-grocers' shops and flowers in the florists' shops, of food in the cafés and something strange and pungent in the shops where the ladies had their hair done. The boy sniffed like a dog, following his mother up the street. A tram came screaming down Hay Street, spitting blue fire from its arm that touched the overhead wires. The sound did something to him inside, like the sound of sirens and drums. (144)

It is from Perth that Rob sends Rick a postcard that turns out to be the only mail Rick receives during his three years in the P.O.W. camp.

> Dear Rick,
> We have come to Perth for two weeks on the train. I hope you will be home soon. I weigh 4 stone 6 lbs 4 oz. I have been sleeping often in your room and I have used your hairbrushes. I hope you don't mind.
> > > > Love
> > > > from
> > > > Rob. (145)

The boy is alive to his senses, and throughout the novel Stow frequently presents the boy's learning to distinguish things according to a collection of sensory images. Geraldton, the town, is different from the country because of its sounds:

> Always the sea, roaring or praying. Always, somewhere, a wind among

leaves, a clank of windmills. Always, somewhere, a rooster crowing, someone hammering, the clop of the baker's horse in the street, a child calling, the whang of the circular saw in the distant woodyard, the far hoot of a lazy train. (124)

. . .

In every season the boy exulted in his senses, in his body. He exulted in the heavy sweetness of jonquils and in the frail scent of tomato leaves; in the harsh rasp of leaves on his skin as he climbed a fig tree, and in the waxy dusty smoothness of the minute date-palm flowers, in the cold sea of early morning, and in the warm sea under the rain. He loved the rough taste of gum leaves and the sweetness in tecoma flowers; the red jewels in pomegranates, and the shells of rainbow beetles in the grey tuart bark. The boy then was little more than a body, a set of sense organs. To himself he had little identity, and to his friends none at all, as they had none to him. (125)

The quotations illustrate the poetic presentation of Rob's growth, but they do not exactly represent the growth of the poetic in Rob. The story is told through the omniscient eye of the narrator, and being omniscient, the narrator can dwell within the mind of Rob or he can distance himself from Rob and observe him. This is Stow's method. He takes a stance similar to the one Joyce takes in his *Dubliners* story "Araby." He is the child grown into the man, and his vision and his voice are those of the man re-creating the child, living again through him, and from his standpoint of distance and maturity, commenting on the stages of development as he presents the child moving through them. In the dramatic scenes, and there are more in this novel than in any of the others, the narrator is one with Rob, and the vision is almost equivalent to that of first person, with the same sort of immediacy and reader involvement. With the changes into omniscience, intimacy is sacrificed and the spell is broken.

Consider the following scene. Rob is wondering about himself and about his town: "He thought often of himself, of who he was, and why. He would repeat to himself his name, Rob Coram, until the syllables meant nothing, and all names seemed absurd. He would think: I am Australian, and wonder why. Why was he not Japanese?" (15). Next comes a description of the town through his eyes. The description ends: "To the north and south the dunes moved in the wind. Each winter the sea gnawed a little from the peninsula. Time was irredeemable. And far to the north was war"

(15). The last two lines shift the reader from the boy's point of view to that of the intruding narrator. In a scene previously quoted, Stow tells the reader that Rob has begun to read the newspaper, "poring over the dark photographs of Hiroshima and Nagasaki, of the bomb itself. . . ." And instead of continuing to concentrate on the boy's view of things, the narrator sermonizes: "It [the bomb] had poisoned the war, poisoned the talk of peace. The negotiations over the surrender dragged on, and the peace to come was tarnished: not a quick, clean joyous peace, like the peace in Europe, but a quibbling guilty peace, too clearly man-made and not God given" (146). With his choice of the omniscient point of view Stow as narrator is certainly within his rights to comment as he chooses, and overall, the narrator intrusions are not numerous, yet these variations in voice from Rob to the narrator and back to Rob again do strike a discordant note.

II *Plot, Characterization, and Rick*

The second half of the novel Stow gives a separate heading: "Rick Home — 1945-1959." The method of presentation continues in the same loosely anecdotal form, with a lyric recreation of Rob's growth in understanding, but now the boy's development is played more immediately against his attempt to understand the changes that have occurred and that continue to occur within Rick. Stow describes the reunion:

The blue eyes that looked at him from the doorway were like light through a magnifying glass, when it is at its brightest and smallest, when paper and leaves begin to smoke.
"Hey," said the man in the door. "Remember me?"
"Yes," the boy said, whispering. "Rick."
He almost winced under the blue gaze. All of Rick seemed to be concentrated in the eyes, with an intensity that ought to have hurt him.
"You knew me," Rick said. "You hadn't forgotten."
"You're — just the same," the boy said, and he felt a gush of gratitude. (155)

It does not take Rob long to realize that he is wrong about Rick, for he is not just the same. Rick cries in the night: "The boy got out of bed and padded across the room. He reached out a clumsy hand

and patted Rick's hair, roughly as if Rick were a puppy. 'Don't cry, Rick,' he said, 'Don't cry'" (162).

As the months pass Rob spends a great deal of time with Rick, with Rick's prison camp mate, Hugh Mackay, and with Rick's girlfriend Jane Wexford. Rick is a constant puzzle to him: why he lies around the house so much, why he examines his body so often in the bedroom mirror, why he doesn't seem to care about things. When his mother says at one point that Rick is "immature," Rob makes out a list of things for which Rick has been criticized and puzzles over it.

The best scenes in the novel are the ones between the "immature" Rick and the adolescent Rob. For Rob the motivation brought about through childish adoration is easily understandable; for Rick the relationship is a freedom from the adult world he has little interest in. Quite serious beneath his humor, he tells Rob, "You're the only person of my age I've got to play with" (170).

As one year passes and then another, Stow focuses more and more on Rick and his problems. Less successful are the scenes dealing with Rick's adult relationships, particularly the scenes involving Rick and his ex-mate Hugh Mackay and Rick's girlfriend Jane Wexford. While Rick cannot fit himself into college and a law career as if nothing has happened, Hugh Mackay marries, takes a house in the suburbs, and dreams no longer of war, as Rick still does, but of golf. "War is another country," Rick at one point tells Rob, and for sensitive men such as Rick, a stay in that other country prevents a readjustment to the sameness in the country that he has left behind. The final answer to Rick's restlessness will come in his expatriation.

The least successful scenes in the novel are those between Rick and Jane Wexford. While in *Tourmaline* Stow presented the emotional conflict between the diviner and Deborah credibly and seemed to have mastered his disability with love scenes, the romantic scenes between Rick and Jane are as wooden and as awkward as those between Patrick and Diana in *The Bystander.* It is almost as if Stow is annoyed with that part of the novel's design that calls for a romantic relationship and he is writing it out of duty rather than from any interest in it. The function of the relationship evidently is to further illustrate Rick's inability to satisfy himself with any of the ordinary ways of making do. Though he finds Jane attractive enough as a woman, she has not been through his experiences of reality in that "other country" of war, and because she is even more of an outsider than is Hugh Mackay, the possibility of meaningful communication is slight. He tries to put on marriage and domesticity as has Hugh Mackay, but finally his ability to pretend that these things are enough breaks down.

While the reasoning behind Stow's use of the love entanglement is sound, his treatment of it is not. The presentation of Jane's unsuccessful attempt at suicide and Rick's consequent decision not to face her again and to leave Australia for good is mechanically rendered, and hardly convincing. Although it would be an overstatement to suggest that the novel is ruined by these scenes, it seems fair to say that the novel does suffer because of the manner in which they are presented.

In fact, the second part of the novel suffers in general with the inclusion of the scenes between Rick and the adults in his world. It suffers because of the shift in focus away from Rob, and Rick and Rob, to an exclusive focus on Rick. This awkwardness in focus could have been handled, perhaps, by an inclusion of Rob in more of the scenes in this section, or by rendering some of them through or partially through his point of view. Even if one grants Stow his method, his shifting of focus, there is still the problem in the development and presentation of the scenes involving the adults, and the critic is right to insist that more should have been done with Hugh, Rick, and Jane.

In the final scene in the novel, when Rick is again with Rob and attempts to explain his malaise to him, Stow is still not as successful as he might be. Rick has made his decision to leave Australia, this "Anglo-Celtic vacuum in the South Seas . . . a good country to be a child in . . . a childish country" (250). He explains further to Rob:

"I can't stand," Rick said, "This — ah, this arrogant mediocrity. The shoddiness and the wowserism and the smug wildboyos in the bars. And the unspeakable bloody boredom of belonging to a country that keeps up a sort of chorus: Relax, mate, relax, don't make the place too hot. Relax, you bastard, before you get clobbered."

The boy stared at the road, aching with uncryable tears. . . . (281)

More statements follow, but for the most part, as the novel ends with Rick leaving Rob alone in a paddock, the reader feels no more satisfied with Rick's explanations than does Rob. The problem is that Stow has insisted on Rick's dissatisfaction, but he has never really shown the "arrogant mediocrity" of Rick's adult world, for the Australian world we have constantly seen is the world of light and color and familial warmth as perceived through the eyes of Rob. Although the reader can understand Rick's problems, the understanding comes more from what the reader brings to the novel than from what Stow brings to the reader.

Rob's development in the second half of the novel, as he grows from ten through thirteen, is presented in the same anecdotal and summary fashion as in the first half. He comes to hate killing animals, he begins to notice girls, he goes on a roundup with Rick and Hugh, he almost drowns. Although Rob's experiences make delightful reading, one finally begins to wish for a tightness that would structure the anecdotes in such a way as to bring conflict into the novel. Perhaps Stow intends for Rick's stance against his homeland to be the element of conflict in this part of the novel, with a subconflict being the breaking of the relationship between Rick and Rob, but since these problems have little to do with Rob's daily goingsout, the reader is left with a multitude of anecdotes that cohere only in the broadest sense of initiation experience.

III *Theme, Symbolism, Humor*

Time, change, the passage from innocence into experience — these are the elements of theme Stow is working with in the novel. The symbol of the merry-go-round, the merry-go-round in the sea, reoccurring at intervals throughout the novel is meant to unify these elements. Stow both begins and ends with this image. To the boy of six, the mast and slanting wires of a barge sunk off the coast have the appearance of a merry-go-round with its top out of the water. Rob refuses to accept his mother's explanation and insists that what he is seeing is a real merry-go-round. A toy merry-go-round is a gift at a children's party; at one point Rob sees a windmill as a merry-go-round. The image of the merry-go-round always represents a romantic unreality for Rob until he faces Rick's decision to leave:

The boy stared at the blue blur that was Rick. Over Rick's head a rusty windmill whirled and whirled. He thought of a windmill that had become a merry-go-round in a back yard, a merry-go-round that had been a substitute for another, now ruined merry-go-round, which had been itself a crude promise of another merry-go-round most perilously rooted in the sea. (283)

Critic Neil McPherson writes of this scene, "At the end Rob has realized that the idealized characters on his merry-go-round, artificially rose-hued, are all parts of a dream world that dissolves under the glare of the outback sun."[2] McPherson looks at Stow's overall use of the merry-go-round symbol, and his conclusion seems a valid one:

Although there is considerable subtlety in the use of this symbol (one can detect that a great amount of effort has gone into its development through the novel), the artifice is not well integrated into the story.... The intelligence of the writer intrudes into the world of the relatively unsophisticated country boy.[3]

Although the integration of the merry-go-round symbol is not stylistically successful, the meaning of the merry-go-round seems clear enough, and whether or not Stow developed the symbol as extensively as he might or integrated it as well as he might is not really of much significance. The novel would work well if there were no merry-go-round symbol at all, and it is not seriously marred by Stow's imperfect use of it.

Nothing has yet been said about the humor in *The Merry-Go-Round in the Sea*, but laughter in the novel is abundant, from gentle humor based on Rob's innocence to a typical kind of humor based on the universals of boyhood. Of the second type, consider the conversation between Rob and his school friends concerning torture. Rob has stuck a thorn in his foot and danced inadvertently onto the hot pavement at the same time.

"Come over here, you drongo."
He leapt into the shade, and stood on one leg to pull the tar off the sole of his foot. "Jiminy, that burns. Hey, that'd be a good way to torture someone."
"I reckon the best way to torture someone," Kevin O'Hara said, "would be to make 'em drink petrol and then drop a match down 'em."
"Aw, the match'd go out."
"No, it wouldn't. They'd be breathing all them fumes."

"What do you want to torture people for?" Graham Martin asked, bored.

"Aw, I don't, really," Kevin said. "Be interesting, though, wouldn't it, to have a Jap to mess around with?" (98)

As for the poetry in the novel, perhaps enough has already been quoted, but at least one final passage will illustrate what Stow does, seemingly with no effort, as he sketches in background for a scene. In the scene that follows, Rob has been staring at Rick, trying to understand him. Looking behind Rick he sees:

In the gum trees along the dry creek that wound almost to the river at Innisfail, cockatoos swirled like torn paper, catching the light. Rising from one tree, they flashed and screeched across the tiger-striped sky to another a quarter of a mile away. They infested the tree like migratory fruit blossom, flapping, tearing, quarrelling. (179)

Maurice Shadbolt, contemporary New Zealand novelist and critic, views *The Merry-Go-Round in the Sea* as Stow's most successful novel, with a revival of his best poetic abilities:

So where to begin again, how to lose those muscle-bound tensions? Stow has found the answer, as so many writers have, in childhood. (Pity the author who begins with childhood, and thereafter has nowhere to retreat.) Out of such retreats have come almost all that is memorable in the literature of childhood....

... *The Merry-Go-Round in the Sea* will probably become a small classic.... For the writer has gone to childhood and discovered a country.[4]

Although the foregoing statements concerning point of view, focus, structure, and symbol would seem to belie my introductory statement that there is little to criticize in the novel, such is not the case. For measured against the achievement in the novel as a whole, the points I indicate for discussion are minor ones rather than significant flaws. They are worth comment, but not worth dwelling on in a summation of the novel. More important is Henry James's standard of "felt life" in the novel, for *The Merry-Go-Round in the Sea* abounds with it. Measured against Stow's other novels, this is the one that truly comes alive, both in terms or character and in terms of poetic impulse.

CHAPTER 7

Act One

R ANDOLPH Stow has published three volumes of poems: *Act One* (1957), *Outrider* (1962), *A Counterfeit Silence* (1969). As with the novels, the poems are specifically Australian in their evocation of land, of sea, of animals, and at the same time universal in subject matter and in allusion, with themes of childhood, of the cruelty and beauty of nature, of love, of death, of rebirth — themes achieved often by dependence on Christian reference and classical allusion. Although the poems remind one of Elizabethan lyric and Scottish ballad, of the French Symbolists, they are not derivative; and the echo serves positively in that it not only indicates the foreground, but, more importantly, the originality of Stow's expansion of it.

I Structure and Poetic Method

Most of the poems in *Act One* were written before Stow was nineteen, many written simultaneously with the writing of *A Haunted Land*. As with the first novel, Stow avoids an outpouring of his personality. He seldom speaks in his own voice, choosing rather to distance himself from his subject to speak through dialogue, through legendary characters, and through fables of his own creation. When in certain poems — "Seashells and Sandalwood," for example — Stow speaks in his own voice, his stance, though personal, is still one of the observer and recorder, rather than that of the confessor or critic.

Stow divides *Act One* into three groups of poems: "Scene One," "Interlude for Voices," and "Scene Two."

II *"Scene One": Private Mythology, Nature, and Children*

The first four poems in "Scene One" are collectively titled "The Hurtful Love," and are individually titled "The Farmer's Tale," "The Fisherman's Tale," "The Gardener's Tale," and "The Shepherdess's Tale." Each poem deals with nature and the participant's encounter with it. In the first poem the farm boy encounters with fear "the lady who a fox is"; he flees, only later to return to passionately wrestle her to the ground in a sexual frenzy, mingling blood and kisses. In "The Fisherman's Tale," the legendary "Rock Man" overturns a ship and, despite the prayers of the mariners, they drown, "...eyes awash with green, crushed to the Rock Man's breast." The gardener in "The Gardener's Tale" awaits "a moth, a girl,/ A frail chimera of all softness —" who arrives as "The strange Marauder." He succumbs to her, is "lost in mists of endlessness, and drifts/ In nights past age." In "The Shepherdess's Tale" a young maiden reclining on capeweed flowers, staring into the clouds, envisions the "Long loping of the wolf and the boy." She is ravished "And out/ Of that sun's cataclysm she learned a hate, torn faced, torn-breasted, lone among her lambs."[1]

With the exception of "The Fisherman's Tale," which is clear and concise, these opening poems depend on a mythology that is perhaps too private to be effective. The mood and idea are clear enough, but the specifics, the fox-lady, the frail chimera, the shepherdess's seducer, are vague.

Six of the next seven poems also deal with nature, specifically a child's encounter with the coast, the sea, the farm, lucious forest, and arid plain. All these poems share in clarity; in Stow's observation of place and object and in his linking of images, he achieves a freshness and a directness that illustrate his power as a poet. In "Seashells and Sandalwood," he writes:

> My childhood was seashells and sandalwood, windmills
> and yachts in the southerly, ploughsares and keels,
> fostered by hills and by waves on the breakwater,
> sunflowers and ant-orchids, surfboards and wheels,
> gulls and green parakeets, sandhills and haystacks, and
> brief subtle things that a child does not realize,
> horses and porpoises, aloes and clematis —
> Do I idealize?
>   Then — I idealize.

The tone is personal — "Do I idealize?" — but not sentimental, and the interjection of the "I" in this poem is the only occasion in the book where the poet seems to speak in his own voice. The "sunflowers and ant-orchids," "gulls and green parakeets," "horses and porpoises," "aloes and clematis" re-create the specificity of place. The images are sensual and abundant in this and most of Stow's poems, and it is this same use of imagery that makes his prose so clear, rich, and pleasing.

"Seashells and Sandalwood" serves as a prelude and introductory summary to the specific encounter with nature that the child has in the poems that follow. In "Sea Children," to the children the sea is a mystery: "...the sea was deeper, and the dive/ Longer, the things to be found in the tangled weed/ Richer and stranger."

"Country Children," which follows, is an initiation poem. The children do more than dream, they observe:

> Country children know more than they know;
> They see the red young bull, his loins on fire,
> Wounding with love the spring of his desire,
> Sowing the savage seed of his cruel youth,
> Eyes staring at the climax.

They observe "the pony, lusty and unwise," the "...slitting up of a rabbit's belly, seeing/ The wet fur never to be born, they know/ The underlying cruelty of being." Stow concludes each of the two stanzas of the poem with the couplet, "For country children know more than they know/ Yet have no worldwise Punch and Judy show."

In "Child Portraits, With Background" Stow indicates the importance of the elements on a child's environment. The child growing up "In Southern Forest" "Hid in the ferns, sought blackberries, watched trout..." and learned that "...life is safe and endless," while the child growing up "On Northern Down" where "the crows cried continually of death/ Over the bare and the dying hills," "...told himself.../ That life is a white bird, screaming through the hills,/ Harsh as brass, fleeting, not to be held." In this place "...spring/ led him where summer sent the sheep to die/ and showed him orchids, eyes of a staring skull."

The beauty and cruelty of nature are companion themes throughout Stow's poems and his novels. It is his recurring images of skulls sprouting flowers, sun-bleached bones, flesh-eating birds that suggest his similarity to the Elizabethan and Jacobean poets and dramatists and to the Scottish balladists. Yet these are not English transplants, for the sun that burns the sand of the outback and the crows that break the silence of the endless spaces are distinctly Australian and real; and they have been the subject of many Australian poets. Deaths in the outback result seldom from man's inhumanity to man, but rather from the hostile forces in nature and the place itself.

Set among the poems of childhood impressions, and illustrating Stow's view of nature, is the ballad "As He Lay Dying." In the first stanza one crow calls to another, "Brother,/ Harvest his eyes, his tongue is mine." In the second stanza two hawks watch the two crows with, "Brother,/ Mine is the sleekest of those." In the final stanza two eagles spot the hawks with "Brother,/ Mark your prey." All this occurs, "As he lay dying." The downs and paddocks that bloom with flowers also ring with death.

In "The Farmer's Boy, with Ladies," and "The Farmer's Parable," Stow returns to the male-female encounter of "The Hurtful Love," the poem sequence that opens the book. The two poems, juxtaposed as they are, illustrate clearly the strengths and weaknesses of the entire volume. In the first, the boy dreams of a lusty encounter with a "fiery negress." They fornicate in the "unholy afternoon" while vixens are "mocking from the bush." However, the girl he walks with, the girl of his "real world," has no sensuality; she has bones as "frail as the bones of a swallow." The poem concludes, "Silent, apart, their love they let no touch/ Unhallow." In this poem Stow treats his subject realistically: the contrast between the pagan sensuality of the aboriginal woman, and the pale, strained "mentalness" of the white girl.

"In "The Farmer's Parable" the subject is the same, young boy meets dusky woman, but the treatment of it is literary rather than direct, and the result is a fuzziness, a lack of clarity. The simple "negress" in the first poem fancifully becomes in the second "a maid/ Brown as a harrowed field." The action occurs not observably in the "moonlit fields" but in a vague place called "this angry land." In the first poem the negress has no need of speech, but in the second, the brown maid feels compelled to repeat a phrase that takes us into literary land. She says, "I am all depth and darkness, I am fire;/ Death is my life, and life is nursed in me." The youth pays no attention to her warning. After a summer and autumn of intercourse, for no explained reason, his head "burst like a pod," and he flounders in a "red and scalding sea."

It is perhaps possible to assign a meaning to the "parable" in the poem, but the overall feeling of vagueness persists. Such is often the case in those poems in the volume in which Stow turns from a direct treatment of his subject to a treatment that relies on a private mythology or an unclearly realized symbol.

These two poems are also illustrative of the recurring fascination Stow has with foxes and with foxlike females. The fox appears in *A Haunted Land* and in many of the poems. The woman is sometimes seen as a fox, "lemon-eyed," "cruel," watchful and fierce. Although it is not always clear what Stow intends the fox to symbolize, it is usually associated with the deceiving, often physically destructive woman.

"Scene One" ends with "Complaint Against Himself." Stow begins, "There is no thing of beauty that this hand,/ Too careful with a pen, has not some way/ Enfeebled, made more concrete, and less rare." The poem is a good one and belies the poet's expression of his own ineptitude at communicating with words.

III   *"Interlude for Voices": Character Studies and Imagery*

"Interlude for Voices" consists of twelve poems. More than half are related from the first person point of view, and the tone in all of them is personal, varying from complaint, to anger, to pleasant wit. There is nothing of the vagueness of symbol or private myth that the reader finds in "Scene One." When there is allusion, as in "David and Abishag," the subject of the allusion, David, speaks as a character in his own voice. Though the "voices" complain of lost love, separation, death, divine injustice, and the losses brought about by age, the complaints are given a freshness by Stow's choice of characters, by his diction, and by his imagery. Consider "Mad Maid's Whim," a poem about a hunchback dressing herself up to scream at God for her deformity: "She has put on a silver gown and gone,/ Crook-backed and crooked-minded, to berate/ The sky in paddocks slow with afternoon." Stow speaks of her "Raging against the seeming mockery/ Of leaves and mudlarks, driving hate to cry/ Hell on harsh God who was and is betraying." Stow concludes, "a hunchback in a blazing gown,/ Striving to smoke a tear in Heaven's eyes.'' The poem is quite visual and the contrasting images of hunchback and silver gown are disturbing; the poem startles the imagination, and the resultant effect is not maudlin.

In "All Hallows' Eve" Stow again resists the trap of sentimentality as he describes the coming to life of a graveyard on Halloween. The reader is reminded of Keats' "The Eve of St. Agnes," with the precision and sensuality of Stow's imagery, and the comparison is a favorable one. The poem begins:

> All Hallows' Eve. The angel on the stone
> Of Mary Johnson spreads his wings;
> White crosses like bare boughs find leaf and bloom;
>   A cherub sings
> From his long-frozen heart a joyful hymn
> And hears it chimed by other cherubim.

If Stow's sensual use of imagery reminds the reader of Keats, it also reminds him of the Pre-Raphaelites as the poet continually fills his poems with color. One of the most charming poems in the volume is the witty and sophisticated verse "The Language of Flowers," subtitled "A Handbook for Victorian Lovers." Stow begins:

> I sent my love clematis. She, walking white
> In her garden, reading Rossetti, veiled her sight
> Under blue eyelids, blushingly comprehended
> Her *mental beauty* was thereby commended.

Here follows a long exchange between the lovers of symbolic flowers: a white rose, an iris, chickweed, gum cistus, yew, rosemary, rue, myrtle, and daisies. The poem is a clever play on the flower convention in English literature, and it illustrates the ease with which the poet uses and manipulates rather than imitates his poetic foreground.

In "Night Sowing," Stow illustrates a versatility in blending figurative and literal language. He commands foxes and lapwings to silence "While Peter loves the earth." Peter, the man on the tractor, "Into the land's dark womb/ The streams of gold seed drain," while

The mist breathed from the ground
To be the bride's coy white
Makes mystic haloes round
The spearing tractor's light.

The positioning of the ideal and the real, the "mist as the bride's coy white" juxtaposed with the modern machine, the tractor with its headlight, is a counterbalance that works well for Stow. He lets us play with romance, but reality is always close at hand.

Stow's economy of diction is seen throughout "Interlude for Voices," but it is particularly exemplified in the six line poem, "Woman's Song, At A Parting." Speaking to her lover, who wants to leave her to seek adventure, the woman ends her thoughts with a couplet, "Go. Go — Fight with the taloned sea./ You leave a deeper strangeness here with me."

IV   "Scene Two": Supercharacters

"Scene Two," containing only eight poems, is shorter than either "Scene One" or "Interlude for Voices." With these eight poems Stow moves beyond his ordinary human beings and their impressions to express his themes through a reliance on representative figures. Some are recognizable as Lucifer, Christ, Adam, Icarus, Tithonus; others are generalized as a "universal warrior," "the first monarch," a frightened child, and a cloistered aristocrat. The representative men illustrate the universals of terror, vanity, sorrow, cruelty, betrayal, death, and immortality. The poems are varied in rhyme and meter, in structure and in length; the shortest poem, "The Universal Warrior," has only six lines, while the longest, "The Continent and the Island," runs to two hundred and thirty-five lines. Stow is both epigrammatic and discursive, and in general he handles both extremes well, though the long "The Continent and the Island" lacks the intensity of the shorter poems.

"The Universal Warrior" is placed alongside "The First Monarch," and both poems show man, whether singular or en masse, to be cruel and stupid. In "The Universal Warrior" Stow writes:

Himself no use to God or to his brothers,
He earns the praise of some by killing others.
HIS TRIUMPHAL ENTRY

> Good citizens, arise, exalt his name.
> Distend with praise his carrion-eating fame.
> HIS GLORIOUS END
> > Long fingering roots find nurture in the urn;
> > In death he takes a more constructive turn.

There is little humor in Stow's poetry, and when one encounters it, it is usually in the form of mockery, as in the last two lines of this poem.

The irony continues in "The First Monarch," as Stow satirizes the various types of spectators. The poem is in two stanzas. The first follows:

> The first great egotist, brass-clad
> And bright in his invincible conceit
> Climbs his proud stupid charger. In the mad
> > Town, in the frozen-minded street
> The crowd goes wild. A noted actress swoons;
> Ecstatically a famous poet hails
> The star set in his navel and the moons,
> The crescent moons, about his fingernails.
> The intellectuals exchange a glance,
> > Pleased to remark a phallus in his lance.

The monarch is inundated as "the cheers batter his thrilling ears." Even "The clergy tries/ to draw his glance with psalms in courtly style." The crowd is wild with pleasure. And then in the final lines, Stow deftly projects the situational irony, as in "The Universal Warrior." He writes, "And meanwhile,/ Forseeing Jezebel, broken in her hair,/ The dogs prick up their ears all round the square."

"Madame Yuan Ying Disoriented" and "The Continent and the Island" are variations of subjects treated by Tennyson in "The Lady of Shalott" and "Tithonus." However, the resemblance in the treatment of the two subjects is slight. Stow compresses Madame Yuan Ying's confrontation with love-sex-reality into thirty lines, whereas Tennyson gives the Lady of Shalott 171. While the Lady of Shalott only looks on Lancelot to bring about her trauma, Madame Yuan Ying allows her young man within her garden walls; and although the result of the experience for Tennyson's lady is death, Stow's lives on in her new "real" world. Stow varies his stanza pattern and rhyme and his poem has nothing of the musical repetition of Tennyson's. His variations are effective, however, particularly when he periodically reduces Madame Yuan Ying's experiences to one line statements.

Stow divides his poem into three parts: (1) a narrative summary of Madame Yuan Ying's present condition: "My lady of the western room sits tearing/ Bright streams of silk between her broken nails." Her nails bloody from rending the material, she grieves for her lost innocence, while "In the lost light there weighs upon her knee/ Intolerably sad, a woven band/ Of gay musicians sprawled beneath a tree." The next verse begins, "And faraway, white waves of orchard land,/ Beside the silken hills, beyond the lake —/ A threaded needle spears the unfinished sand." (2) Madame Yuan Ying speaks of the admission of the stranger into her garden and asks:

> Where is the quiet world, the silken world,
>   Where is the song, oh you harsh time in spate?
> Where is the simple real and unreal world
>   I knew before I opened up my gate?

(3) The narrator concludes the poem in a single couplet: "Lady, outside your autumn room the night/ Grows, and there is no way back to light." "Madame Yuan Ying Disoriented," one of the earliest of Stow's published poems, is a fine example of the poet's work. It illustrates his use of the image, his succinctness, and his clarity.

"The Continent and the Island," with 232 lines, is the longest poem in the volume, and as such is a departure from Stow's usual brevity, a departure that illustrates very well the poet's ability to create a lengthy work without losing himself in verbosity or losing the impact of his precision in imagery. Unlike Tennyson's "Tithonus," which is a monologue involving only the aged Tithonus, Stow's poem involves three speakers: a narrator, who is the "son" of the old grasshopper-man; Tithonus; and Endymion. The "son" questions Tithonus, who has been given perpetual life without perpetual youth, Tithonus who is so old that he "rasps dry as leaves," and he questions Endymion, who has been given perpetual youth but a life restricted only to sleep. Unlike Tennyson's Tithonus who longs for death, for release, Stow's old man clings to life, wretched as it is. To the questioning "son," he says, "But shall I die? No, while there be one bone/ shall hold from crumbling, breath shall breath pursue;/ You call me doomed: no more, my son, than you." The "son's" reaction is one of repulsion, "And I stood there/ Contemptuous of his misery and age."

Seeking further advice on the question of aging and death, he comes to the sleeping Endymion. Entering Endymion's dream state, the "son" listens to the aged youth's advice not to cling to physical life, not to fear the creeping Tithonus who brings old age and death with him. Endymion sees a great harmony beyond this life, "the moment's falsity," and advises, "...because I love you I say — Die./ Go, cast your anchor off, you yet may fly."

"The Continent and the Island" brings together the companion themes of "Scene Two" and of the volume as a whole, themes of beauty and ugliness, youth and age, death and immortality. Of Tithonus, Stow writes:

> Here he rots and here he moves;
> In the corrupting sun his belly drags
> Over the ruinous marble's whorls and grooves.
> And loves its smoothness as the sad flesh sags
> With sickening age between his needle-legs.

But about the beautiful boy

> The breeze
> Blows soft and hot with poppy-breath, the grass
> Steams with green warmth
> . . .
> A crane stands tall in the shadow of a fern
> By a stream where gold and silver waters run.

Clearly Endymion's advice is also the poet's. In this world, Stow's world, order gives way to disorder, security to terror, beauty to decay and death. Yet if, as Endymion says, "Every man must carry his death within him," there is a chance for a bit of life beyond the grave. In "A Fancy For His Death," which ends the volume, Stow expresses this possibility:

> Here is one more than sweat on lichened stone;
> For now the bronze-flowered poison bush shall rise

> Bursting in sparks and flaming from his thighs,
> And he is made perpetual with the sun.

Act One illustrates the wide range of Stow's abilities. He is comfortable with the specifics of the Australian countryside and character; he is equally capable of adapting for his own uses both mythological figures and traditional poetic conventions. He moves easily among the conventional stanza patterns and uses unconventional ones when he chooses.

The critics have been fairly consistent in their praise of *Act One*. In 1957 it was awarded the Gold Medal by the Australian Literature Society.

CHAPTER 8

Outrider

*O*utrider, Randolph Stow's second volume of poems, was published in 1962, five years after *Act One,* and was strikingly
illustrated with paintings by Sidney Nolan. It is an uneven achievement, and though it contains a number of good poems, it leaves the
reader, especially if he has come to it directly after a reading of the
first volume, wondering as to the merit of the changes the poet has
made in his approach. The outstanding characteristic of the major-
ity of poems in *Act One* is the directness of Stow's treatment of his
subject, the highly visual quality of his words, the creation of an
imagery that illuminates and gives clarity to his thoughts. Although
the best poems in *Outrider* continue in this manner, too many are
mental in a way that produces a haziness, a vagueness that, because
it seems deliberately contrived, vexes rather than intrigues the
reader. Furthermore, there is often a verbosity, a "wordwreath,"
to use Stow's term, that lessens the effect of the startling image or
single line that is the reason for the poem.

Stow divides the volume into two parts, the first with fourteen
poems, the second with ten.

Part One
I   *Realism, Satire, Romance*

The book begins happily enough, with four distinctly Australian
poems: "Dust," "In Praise of Hillbillies," "The Utopia of Lord
Mayor Howard," and "The Wild Duck's Nest."

"Dust" is a satirical poem about a housewife who, tired of fighting dust, "spurned her broom and took a train." She is not heard
from again. The poem records in surrealistic fashion what happens
in her house as dust takes over: "Never such heath as flowered on
the virgin slopes/ of the terrible armchairs. Never convolvulus/

119

brighter than that which choked the china dogs." The event is so notable that "a photographer came from *The West Australian,* and ten/ teenage reportresses." Botany teachers are curious too, but the neighbors, fearful of nature, of such a thing happening to them, "slept behind sealed doors, with feather/ dusters beside their beds."[1]

"In Praise of Hillbillies" humorously describes three hillbillies and gives a verse of song by each. "Harry, who has two squeeze-boxes, can yodel/ high as the sun." Jabulmara sings of "...tall/ Hellenic stockmen cut down in their primes,/ far from the Flying Doctor," and "Kev, in the country of the myall tree,/ crashes a plastic pick across the strings" and sings of "broken-hearted sheilas left behind/ in cities he may never know."

"The Utopia of Lord Mayor Howard" begins with a clipping from *The West Australian* in which Lord Mayor Howard wants to replace the trees on the corner with "neat rose gardens" because the trees have "grown so tall that they had lost all their attraction." The poem that follows the clipping is a satire on the result of the mayor's taste. Trees are felled all about because "Nothing shall be taller than Lord Mayor Howard/ but insurance buildings." Those opposing the mayor are forced to flee because of a rumor that some "had been seen to spit on roses." In exile the tree lovers, rose haters form a religion known as "anti-Rosaceanism." People lonely for trees join the rebels, so many that Stow says in conclusion, "we half expect to see Lord Mayor Howard."

In "The Wild Duck's Nest" two men "hunting a bird to drop, a beast to kill," come upon "nine grey-white eggs laid warmly in a bowl of down." As the men stand over the nest imagining some nest robber to come, "half-hating/ the sleek thief, somewhere waiting for his day," kangaroos run crashing through the brush in fear. The men can see no enemy until they catch each other's vision and see themselves as the killers they are. "'There are two men.' A thousand birds/ rose screaming at the words. And all beasts cowered."

The four poems placed at the outset of the volume suggest a poet moving beyond the romantic, generalized, and sometimes literary concerns of *Act One.* In the first volume Stow places himself at some distance from his subject, looking backward to childhood, looking further backward to historical and mythical figures, dancing about cleverly with conventions. But with these first four poems in *Outrider,* the poet has removed the mask and shortened the distance and comments in a direct and personal voice on the contemporary experience. He is sure enough of himself to relax his tone of high seriousness in the first three of these poems, to play satirically, humorously with his subject. In "Dust" the theme of nature versus man that is frequently worked with in such a serious manner in *Act One* is reduced to the playful level of a housewife relinquishing her broom. The stupidity and cruelty of man presented in "The Universal Warrior" and "The First Monarch" is treated comically in "The Utopia of Lord Mayor Howard." Man philosophizing on his troubles and lamenting his fate is turned into the hackneyed moans of hillbillies. And in "The Wild Duck's Nest" it is not nature that is seen as destructive, frightening, but ironically, realistically, man.

If all the poems in *Outrider* resembled these first four — resembled them in a technique that produces a clear, controlled communication of experience — then it would be possible to designate *Outrider* as an illustration of the poet's movement in a definite direction, primarily toward realism. However, no such generalization is possible, for in a number of the poems that follow, Stow returns to a romantic presentation of his subject.

Romantic treatments of shipwreck and death reappear in this volume in the poems "The Embarkation" and "The Ship Becalmed." The destructive nature of time is recounted once more in "Ruins of the City of Hay," "At Sandalwood," and "The Ghost at Anlaby." Among the poems of repeated themes, "The Ghost at Anlaby" is worth pausing with, for it illustrates Stow's combining of romantic subject and realistic technique, a combination that works well for him. In the poem an Edwardian ghost returns to the estate, Anlaby, and relives a typical afternoon: "Now sulkies come haunting softwheeled down the leaves." The house and lawn fill with "antwaisted, hamsleeved, bellskirted ladies/ crossing the lawns with fishtailed racquets/ intent on tennis." As for the men, "Below the willows/ Tom Roberts squatters, George Lambert ladies," referring to Australian painters of the day. There are lilacs, wisteria, crabapple. The ghost is remorseful at seeing again such an afternoon and thinks, "Once time was a sportsman, and I the quarry,/ who now would sleep with death, for sleep's kind sake." The ghost concludes the picture: "Among wraiths of cigar smoke,/ with rib-nudging stories I died before telling/ I shall go haunting in search of a friend, a friend." "The Ghost at Anlaby" is elegant and poignant, with the grace and sensual appeal of "The Language of Flowers" and "All Hallows' Eve" from *Act One.*

II *Clarity, Tone*

Two poems that illustrate the vagueness that is inherent in numerous poems in *Outrider* are "The Land's Meaning" and "Strange Fruit." "The Land's Meaning" is dedicated to Sidney Nolan, illustrator of the volume, and is one of Stow's offerings in a long line of Australian poems dealing with the problems of the early explorers of the outback. "The Land's Meaning" records the report of a returned explorer who has after forty years of being alone learned the value of companionship.

The problems in the poem involve clarity and tone. A lack of clarity becomes apparent when one attempts to understand two epigrams in the poem, and it comes from the overall organization of the poem. Stow begins the poem with the epigram: "The love of man is a weed of the waste places./ One may think of it as the spinifex of dry souls." The metaphor is unclear. I suppose the meaning is that "waste places" teach one the necessity of brotherly love, or perhaps that love grows with a weedlike abundance in waste places. The placing of the second epigram so close to the first adds to the confusion. If the poet starts with an idea, the reader rightly expects that what follows will illustrate the idea, but when the illustration is itself interrupted with another problematic epigram, then the result is an even greater vagueness. Stow follows the opening epigram with the statement that though he has not "made the trek to the difficult country/ where it [love] is said to grow," reports come back "that the mastery of silence/ alone is empire. What is God, they say,/ but a man unwounded in his loneliness?"

Coupled with the first epigram, I suppose the second means that God is superior to man, only because he can stand without companionship; he is "unwounded" by loneliness. And yet a question arises concerning the state toward which one should aspire: to be Godlike, a "loner," or to learn from the waste places brotherly love. Stow concludes the poem with the report of one who has returned from the "waste places":

"And I came to a bloke all alone like a kurrajong tree.
And I said to him: 'Mate — I don't need to know your name —

let me camp in your shade, let me sleep, till the sun goes down.'''

And in this statement of need, do we have the land's meaning?

Further lessening the impact of the poem is a change in tone. To illustrate the horror of the outback, the man now returned speaks of the animals' refusing to enter deeper into it: "The third day cockatoos dropped dead in the air"; the unwary man is enveloped in the waste, but to record this horror, Stow abruptly changes his tone, with the speaker punning, "I was bushed for forty years."

Part of the problem in "The Land's Meaning" is inherent in Stow's general method. He starts with his idea and then invents an illustration. He is far more successful in other poems, "The Wild Duck's Nest," for example, when the specific incident, realistically recorded, leads to the suggestion of the idea. Incident creating idea works better than idea creating incident.

"Strange Fruit" illustrates a tendency often found in contemporary poetry, but one usually avoided by Stow, the publication of a poem too private in meaning to be understood by the general reader. Of "Strange Fruit" all that can be stated clearly is that one person is following another on horseback; the follower is afraid to face the other in the daylight, "fearing your quester's ear, that might interpret/ what sings in my blood; your eye that might guess my fever." The narrator describes himself as "the country's station; all else is fever." The reader is not given enough information to interpret this private summation. The narrator continues, watching the person sleeping by the fire:

Alone for an hour, in a thicket, I reached for strange fruit.
Now you sleep by the fire. And these are my true eyes
that glare from the swamps. And the rattling howl in the gullies
is my true voice. That cries: *You shall try strange fruit.*

What has happened, what is about to happen, and the cause of the narrator's fever is not known; and although ambiguity skillfully designed can be enjoyable in poetry, vagueness without the proper signposts is not.

Part Two

III *Problematic World*

The problems found in Part One are found also in Part Two. The reader strains toward meaning, only to be disappointed by the over-all vagueness of the poem, or by the conclusion to the poem which is itself unclear. These problems are particularly apparent in "Kàpisim! O Kiriwina," "Convalescence," and "Outrider," the poem that bears the volume's title. Absent in the second half of the volume is satire or any relief from seriousness. The poems in Part Two picture a ruinous world in which youth passes, "The Dying Chair"; a homestead is destroyed, "Sleep"; love is difficult, "Landscapes"; sickness brings madness, "Convalescence," "The Calenture"; and ventures from one's native land bring unhappiness or a vow of silence, "Landfall," "Outrider."

Four representative poems from Part Two are "Sleep," "Endymion," "The Calenture," and "Landfall."

In an apostrophe suggestive of Sir Philip Sidney, the poet addresses Sleep, but in this case the speaker is a burned-out stockman who praises the healing powers of sleep. The stockman's address to Sleep frames his reflections on the ongoing tragedy that has caught him up. The poem begins with the apostrophe: "Sleep: you are my homestead, and my garden;/ my self's stockade; identity's last fortress. . . ." Then follow three stanzas in which the man recounts his tragedy. He begins: "All day I have stood the siege, and my hands are shaking;/ my paddocks are charred and fuming, my flocks are slaughtered,/ my lands mirror the moon in desolation." When, with the coming of night and the attacking tribes "like smoke, seep campward," the man bars "the wall-slits with jarrah shutters" and puts aside his rifles, he addresses sleep once more: "Sleep: who are silence; make me a hollow stone/ — filled with white blowing ash, and wind, and darkness." Following this address are three two line stanzas of his thoughts about his tragedy. The poem closes with a final apostrophe to sleep.

The poem is well-structured, with changes in thought cleverly integrated. The problem with the poem, however, is in the questionable sentiment. The stockman, surrounded by dead flocks and charred ruins, with no promise that the slaughtering tribes will not return, begins with an unconvincing statement of brotherhood: "So far, so sweet, I know I shall some day love them. . . ." He concludes with "and man I mourn; till the hurts are as wrongs in childhood/ — and a child forgets; though he weep, asleep, forever. . . ." Not only is the unprepared for benevolence unbelievable, but the final statement is unclear. What is the meaning of "though he weep, asleep, forever"?

Stow works well with the two line stanza, and he uses it again in "Endymion." Unlike his treatment of Endymion in *Act One,* the Endymion in this poem is a modern man looking at a moon deromanticized by science. He begins:

> My love, you are no goddess: the bards were mistaken;
> no lily maiden, no huntress in silver glades.
>
> You are lovelier still by far, for you are an island;
> a continent of the sky, and all virgin, sleeping.

The revelations of science have not destroyed the moon's beauty. The speaker, who will go "to annex your still mountains with patriotic ballads,/ to establish between your breasts my colonial hearth" sees a new beauty. He will go to her, "forgetting all trees, winds, oceans and open grasslands,/ and forgetting the day for as long as the night shall last." The poem is fresh, the imagery clear, and there is no cloudy philosophical statement pressed upon the reader.

Stow includes a page of notes at the end of *Outrider* to explain certain uncommon words or terms found in the poems. *Calenture,* in "The Calenture," he defines as "A disease incident to sailors within the tropics, characterized by delirium in which the patient, it is said, fancies the sea to be green fields, and desires to leap into it." "The Calenture," a poetic description of the disease, is one of the finest poems in the volume. It works where "The Land's Meaning" fails because it is coherent. The speaker is a specific man, who speaks of his specific illness, and having knowledge of it, determines to avoid its danger, the suicide that the illusion invites. Stow writes the poem in the first person, having the man tell of his predicament: "Abandoned I heave in fever, the calenture's heretic pupil." Not wanting to succumb, he prays, "Mary, star of the ocean: confound all witchcraft so lovely." He reminds himself, "gentle indeed though the grass is," he is a seaman and should not be attracted to the land. He concludes: "I am not deceived, I find, by the waving grass; whose scent,/ crushed out by tranquil sleepers, crowds every porthole." In addition to the sensual nature of the imagery and its clarity, "The Calenture" is a personal poem that creates a sense of sympathy for the sick man, and because of this, the reader is more directly involved in this poem than in most others of the volume.

"Landfall," the final poem in the volume, is also related in the first person. We assume the speaker to be the poet, but he need not be. We assume the place to be the poet's home in Western Australia, but it need not be. We assume the silence the speaker predicts to refer to a poetic reticence, but it need not. The poem is a fitting one to end with, for it illustrates the best of the poet's craftsmanship. The poem is both specific in setting and universal; realistic in detail, yet romantic in concept; clear in meaning, yet intriguing in implication. I quote it in full:

> And indeed I shall anchor, one day — some summer morning
> of sunflowers and bougainvillaea and arid wind —
> and smoking a black cigar, one hand on the mast,
> turn, and unlade my eyes of their cargo;
> and the parrot will speed from my shoulder, and white yachts glide
> welcoming out from the shore on the turquoise tide.
>
> And when they ask me where I have been, I shall say
> I do not remember.
>
> And when they ask me what I have seen, I shall say
> I remember nothing.
>
> And if they should ever tempt me to speak again,
> I shall smile, and refrain.

CHAPTER 9

A Counterfeit Silence

A Counterfeit Silence, published in 1969, is Randolph Stow's third volume of verse. The title is taken from a passage in Thornton Wilder's *The Bridge of San Luis Rey:* "Even speech was for them a debased form of silence; how much more futile is poetry, which is a debased form of speech."[1] The book is divided into three parts: *Juvenilia,* poems written from 1954–1956; *Outrider,* 1957–1962; and *Stations,* 1962–1966. With the exception of "For One Dying" in *Juvenilia,* all the poems in the first two parts were published previously in *Act One* and *Outrider,* Stow's first two volumes of poetry. *Stations* adds nine new poems, three of which are poetic sequences.

The themes of the new poems repeat concerns from the first volumes: time and change, "A Feast"; the effect of the land, "The Singing Bones," "Stations"; peopled seascapes, "A Wind From the Sea," "Western Wind, When Will Thou Blow"; separation from home, "Ishmael," "Persephone"; sequential poetic interpretations of the Australian prisoner of war experience in Thailand, "Thailand Railway"; and the themes of the *Tao Teh Ching* in "The Testament of Tourmaline."

I Short Poems

Stations begins with "A Feast," a first person narrative poem in which the speaker presents two realities, one civilized, one primitive. Stow precedes his poem with a quotation from *Guide to Burleigh House,* "Also in the room are Cromwell's boots, and on a refectory table, a mummified cat, an Abyssinian lyre, and other items of interest." The quotation, itself so specific in its singling out of things, reads like a line from Stow's own verse. The poet uses the line from the guidebook to place himself:

127

> Stumbling on lovely lumber, old rites, stud liquor,
> soothed by the sweet traditional fibs of actors,
> from the sort of limbo I live in I discern
> vistas of gentlemen raising their heads to give reasons
> why the picture, poem, architrave, sonata,
> should be, in fact, what the best books say they are.[2]

He comments on himself, which is at the same time a comment on those critics who judge what is valuable: "Lord, I am not worthy. Let me pig it a while/ with a people which is not redeemed from time." Reflecting in this way, he remembers "an old dark man in Mwatwa village/ who built a new sago-leaf homestead, hacking the uprights/ from growing wood." The "gable-boards took root" and the poet thinks of the "old man and his old wife, cross-legged and smiling,/ their burgeoning and perennial house behind them."

Two experiences, two "civilizations," and the narrator in the "limbo" between, an observer of each. He is uncomfortable in the English setting where past experience is already preserved and evaluated, and prefers to "pig it a while/ with a people ... not redeemed from time." "I am not worthy," he says, the implication being "worthy" to define clearly what in life is so valuable as to be singled out and preserved as significant. The title of the poem, "A Feast," suggests the view of life that allows the narrator to draw both experiences together. In the "feast" of life many things are valuable, and thus the "unworthy" critic, the narrator, can observe the "mummified cat, an Abyssinian lyre," from Burleigh House and place alongside them his preservation in memory of "an old man and his old wife, cross-legged and smiling,/ their burgeoning and perennial house behind them."

In what way is value defined? It is an open-ended question the poet leaves with us. As in "Landfall," the poem that closes *Outrider,* the voice in this poem is direct and personal. There is no poetic mask, no diffusion of meaning; and as with "Landfall," the experience is easily seen in universal terms.

The poet turns again to his homeland in the two short poems "The Singing Bones" and "Ishmael" and in the long sequence of poems "Stations." "The Singing Bones" begins with a quotation from Barcroft Boake's bush ballad: "Out where the dead men lie." The poem is a tribute to the explorers of the Australian outback, both physical and spiritual, men such as Leichhardt, Gibson,

Gordon, and Boake. Stow writes: "Out there/ its sand-enshrined lay saints lie piece by piece,/ Leichhardt by Gibson...." He continues in the following stanza: "No pilgrims leave, no holy-days are kept/ for these who died of landscape." The men "...were all poets, so the poets said," dreaming their dreams. But reality shows a brutal end for each of them: "Gordon died happy, one surf-loud dawn, shot through the head,/ and Boake astonished, dead, his stockwhip round his throat." The poet can still hear their singing bones, "their glum Victorian strain./ A ritual manliness, embracing pain/ to know; to taste terrain their heirs need not draw near."

In "Ishmael" Stow turns from the historical past to the present, with a voice longing for home: "Oasis. Discovered homeland. My eyes drink at your eyes./ Noon by noon, under leaves, my dry lips seek you." The speaker would like to forget, to be relieved of "this encumbering/ tenderness," and he calls

> to mind to mould the mind, inviting
> desert and sky to take me, wind to shape me
> strip me likewise of softness, strip me of love,
> leaving a calm regard, a remembering care.

There is a tension in "Ishmael," in "Persephone," and in "Outrider" from the preceding volume, that suggests the inward struggle of the poet separated from his homeland. The struggle is further suggested and explained in the long poem "Stations."

II *"Stations"*

"Stations" was commissioned by the Poetry Book Society of Great Britain and was performed as a part of the Commonwealth Festival of Arts, 1965. The poem is subtitled "Suite for Three Voices and Three Generations." The voices are those of "The Man," "The Woman," and "The Youth," and the time span of three generations — three poems for each — stretches from the Australian Colonial Period to the time of the world wars. The voices speak in nine separate poems. (1) "A Man is Like That" — In Part One, the man speaks first, telling of the dream that causes one to leave home for a new land. He tells of one who leaves home, "And seas and sands will wound and mould him, and strange races/ teach arrogance and loneliness and shame." (2) "The Dark

Women Go Down'' — The woman speaks of the aboriginal notion of procreation: "The dark women go down to the haunted pool./ They speak to the children, the spirits, the yet-unborn." The woman continues, "I have robbed from the starving women, I have gone down/ to the pool of children and stolen, I have conceived/ a tall blond son, and the pools and the land are his." The aborigine culture is destroyed; the white mother "conspires, endures," knowing she will "flow in my tall blond sons, in my tender daughter." (3) "There Was a Time" — The youth remembers nothing of the fights with the aborigines, "when this warm-reeking woolshed was a fortress." Rather, he says, "I remember only peace, the predicted harvest." (4) "Forever to Remain" — The man speaks again. The problems of the second generation are less perilous than those of the first. The man says, "And I must serve my generation's sentence:/ *forever to remain,* forever meeting/ the altered eyes, forever building for ever." (5) "My Wish for the Land" — If the man plans "Athens and Camelot," the woman turns to dreams of material and social comfort: "My wish for my husband is that he read Tennyson./ My wish for my daughter is that she be interesting/ and capture a million acres." And later she says, "My wish for my house is that linen be Irish/ and tableware sterling. . . ." (6) "Here Also Let the Troubling Dream" — The youth dreams of the social destiny of the new land:

> Here then, in this most bare, most spare, least haunted,
> least furnished of all lands, we are to foster
> greenly the dream, the philadelphic idyll,
> and in good faith and in good heart dream on.

(7) "The Earth and World Besiege Us" — In Part Three the third generation is beset with problems of drought and crop failure at home and is once again put in touch with the problems of Europe, the problems of economic privation and war. The man speaks:

> The earth and world besiege us. Destitution
> waits round the corner of a season, only
> because across two seas a market toppled,
> a law fell flat.

Of Europe, he says, "We have lived to witness/ the brotherhood of man: the starving brothers/ scrambling for crusts on a crumbling shanty star." (8) "The Garden Runs Wild" — The woman watches her world change: "The garden runs wild. The young men arm and go./ There have been strangers mustering at our gates/ and fears in homesteads. War blacks out the land." (9) "The Grief of Younger Brothers" — The youth, left behind while his older brother fights and is killed, speaks:

> The grief of younger brothers does not heal.
> It aches unspoken. I was not with those
> who stormed the ridge or shattered in the sky;
> I was the child who lived that they might die.

Left alone, grieving "in the once shared room," the youth questions, "'The proud rider lies still/ and must be avenged.' But who — who must I kill?" The woman ends the poem with the woman's original thought: "Across the uncleared hills of the nameless country/ I write in blood my blood's abiding name."

"Stations" is the best of Stow's long poems. It is rich in feeling, distinct and economical in its historical summary of attitudes and emotions. The diction is simple, the ideas clearly expressed, the tone personal and sympathetic.

III *"Thailand Railway," "From the Testament of Tourmaline"*

The two long poems that follow and complete the volume are not as successful, possibly because the poet does not come to his material as directly as with "Stations." The first of these, "Thailand Railway," is a recreation of the jungle experiences of Australian prisoners of war, experiences related in part to Stow by the writer Russ Braddon, and it is to Braddon that Stow offers the poem: "Your memories, not mine; a debt to repay a debt."

"Thailand Railway" is composed of ten short poems, with such titles as "The Jungle," "Slaves," "The Track," "The Enemy." The poems tell the hardships suffered by the prisoners as in the deep jungle they build a railroad "to link Bangkok with Rangoon," to link "slave and slave." The most poignant lyrics describe the mateship of the prisoners as they watch each other die of starvation and disease, helping each other as they can. In "The Sleepers" the prisoner observes, "My neighbour moans in his sleep, and I stretch my arm,/ and he sighs and quietens under my arm like a child,/ gaunt cheek on hand." In "The Fire" Stow describes in couplets the burning of the dead prisoners. "The bonfire blazes, day and night./ What can keep the fire so bright?" The answer comes in the next couplet. "Skin and bone, flesh and hair./ Many a brother have I flung there." There is a short poem in praise of hands: "hands raising water to dying lips,/ doing the work of the dying"; and in "Bring Your Piano" the speaker records the courageous voices of the prisoners as they unite in song. The poem ends with "The Children," and in this lyric the narrator speaks of the comforting vision of children at home, free and at ease. It is this vision that lessens the mental anguish of the soldiers.

> For, in the end, what charge is there to lay
> but this: Be children still, in peace, for ever?
>
> Children: as we would reach out to the orphan,
> think of the childless dead, and be our sons.

Stow re-creates these same experiences in his novel *The Merry-Go-Round in the Sea.* Rick Maplestead is witness to the loss of mates and the burning of the dead, and the effect of his experience is dramatically detailed. Free of couplet rhymes and the stricture of compression, the prose account is more satisfying than this poetic one.

The final poem in the volume is titled "From THE TESTAMENT OF TOURMALINE Variations of Themes of *The Tao Teh Ching.* The reference in the title to the testament of Tourmaline is a reference to Tom Spring, a character in Stow's novel *Tourmaline,* and the testament is his account of his beliefs to The Law, the man who narrates the story in *Tourmaline.*

Stow's long poem consists of twelve short poems, each a re-creation of the substance of thought in twelve numbered passages in the text of *The Tao Teh Ching.* As an example of what Stow does, let us look at Passage Five in *The Tao Teh Ching.* It begins: "1 – Heaven and earth do not act from (the impulse) any wish to be benevolent." Point 2 begins: "May not the space between heaven and earth be compared to a bellows?"[3] The first and last stanzas of Stow's Number 5 follow:

> A smith at work
> does not consult the iron.

> Passionless, silent,
> he forms it to his pattern.
>
> . . .
>
> What can be empty
> yet ever and all replenishing?
> Under the bellows
> blazes the world's forge-fire.

It is interesting to compare the original and the poet's transformation of it, but the only criterion for judgment is the poem itself. Though individual stanzas are striking, Stow's poem as a whole does not catch the imagination. One has the feeling that the desire to reproduce the thought takes precedence over the impulse to create a poem.

The poems that work best are, characteristically, those that interpret the philosophy of Taoism by making reference to the land and its properties. The general water imagery of Taoism is made specific in the lines, "The red land rises from the ocean/ erodes, returns; the river runs earth-red/ staining the open sea." In Number 16 the Chinese philosopher speaks generally of the vegetable world that grows and then returns to its root, returning to a kind of stillness. In Stow's Number 16, the plant is the myall and the image becomes specific:

> Deep. Go Deep.
> As the long roots of myall
> mine the red country
> for water, for silence.

The final stanza, which closes the poem and the volume, Number 81, refers to language. The language is itself a link to the land, the land that has to such a great extent produced the language for Stow's poetry.

> Words well and sperm jets, sap mounts and fountains flow
> from dark to light, from Tao to the lasting land
>
> that my words commend, whose names are sweet in my mouth.
> In the silence between my words, hear the praise of Tao.

CHAPTER 10

Other Works

I Midnite

PERHAPS the biggest surprise in the body of Stow's writing is *Midnite* (1967). It is a surprise because while most of Stow's writing, with the exception of a brief scene or a few satirical poems, is serious, *Midnite* is whimsical and delightfully funny. It is not the first of Stow's books about children; there are Keithy Farnham in *The Bystander* and Rob Coram in *The Merry-Go-Round in the Sea*, but it is the first of his books in which the child's encounter with the world is a continuously funny one; and it is the first of Stow's works written for children.

Midnite, "The Story of a Wild Colonial Boy," is set in Australia in the mid-nineteenth century and recounts the adventures of a "rather stupid," good-natured seventeen year old boy, who, orphaned with the death of his father, takes the advice of Khat, a talking Siamese cat, who suggests that he become a famous bush-ranger, stealing horses and cattle and robbing coaches. The boy calls himself Captain Midnite and forms a gang consisting of the animals about the house, Khat, who is "the brains"; Dora, "a rather silly cow, who was not nearly so young as she thought she was"; Red Ned, a noble horse; Gyp, a sheepdog; and Major, an irritable, crafty cockatoo. The book is made up of Midnite's adventures, which land him in jail numerous times, and which involve him in romance, exploration, a discovery of gold, even an audience with Queen Victoria.

Like so many good children's books, *Midnite* is for the adult reader a satire, and a really humorous one as Stow laughs at many of the aspects of Australian life that he has elsewhere treated seriously. The subtitle of the book, "The Wild Colonial Boy," is an allusion to the popular ballad of the same name and indicates Stow's intention from the outset, to burlesque Australian Romantic pretensions. Held up for comic examination are mateship, colonial social affectations, legal justice, the gold rush, Queen Victoria, and the outback in which Midnite encounters the German explorer Voss, who, talking in backward syntax, names the place "the Cosmic Symbolical Desert" — a satiric nod to Patrick White.

For children, *Midnite* is an adventure story of the best sort as the animals plot and scheme and rescue Midnite. And as in most children's books, the escapades of the hero teach him morals, in Midnite's case, the dangers of lying, card playing, alcohol, and stealing. For children and adults alike, *Midnite* is a charming book, full of grace and wit and laughter.

II *"Magic"*

"Magic," published in *Commonwealth Short Stories* (1966), is a dramatic re-creation of a myth of the Trobriand Islands (near New Guinea), a myth concerning the strongest of their sexual taboos, the incestuous attraction of a brother and sister. The Trobriander believes that love is a product of magic, and that one who has magic can make love happen, but inherent in the use of magic is also the possibility of accident or misuse. The most feared love attraction is that of the brother and sister. As a partial protection against this event, the brother and sister are discouraged from playing together as children, and then, as the boy grows up, he leaves the home to sleep in bachelor quarters. Stow's story is of the accidental misapplication of magic as the girl Soulava spills the magic mixture on her head and in madness and lust relentlessly pursues her brother Lalami. Lalami succumbs and in knowing that their consummation will bring death, the couple lie in a cave in each other's arms, awaiting the end.

"Magic" is an illustration of all that is good about Stow's writing. The words are simple, the sentences short, the images colorful. The dialogue is made up of short statements, some of which are repeated as a kind of refrain. The total effect of this economy is a re-creation of a primitive world half asleep in lime gourd, coral, fowl-dung, poinsettia, palm shade, torpor, and lethal magic.

III *"Dokónikan"*

"Dokónikan" is the second of Stow's stories set in the Trobriand Islands and based on island myths. According to the author's note at the end of the story, his "Dokónikan" combines two versions of the myth told to him by islanders.[1]

Dokónikan as a baby delighted his mother and sister, delighted them, that is, until he began to cut teeth. He continued to cut teeth until he had four rows of them and a mouth like a shark. Stow writes, "His mother still loved him, but she had to refuse him her breast."[2] As Dokónikan grew up he had only his sister for companionship. He tried to make magic to bring himself a lover, but no one had taught him how, and his magic failed. Deciding that if he could replace his ugly spirit with another's beautiful spirit, he could be happy, he looked with love at his charming niece and ate her. This was the beginning of a bad habit that did not stop until Dokónikan had eaten everyone on the island except his sister and two others. Eventually his sister, who had eaten a few people herself, went off for sago pudding to change her diet and left Dokónikan. He was alone and miserably unhappy.

The end comes for Dokónikan as Bulutúkwa, one of the remaining islanders, makes a strong magic and sends her handsome hero-son Tudáva to kill Dokónikan. The magic is beautiful, and Dokónikan, seeing the handsome Tudáva, thinks he himself has grown beautiful, and delightfully drunk with magic, dies with a smile on his face. The head is to be cooked by Bulutúkwa and sent to frighten to death the uncle who has left her behind on Dokónikan's island.

"Dokónikan," like "Magic," is gracefully written; but the sense of tragedy in "Magic" is replaced with a bit of playfulness in "Dokónikan" as Stow matter-of-factly records Dokónikan's eating habits. The style is in harmony with the way in which a child or a primitive might relate such things: acts of cannibalism are quite pleasant in myths and fairy tales.

IV   *"Eight Songs For a Mad King" and*
"Miss Donnithorne's Maggot"

"Eight Songs For a Mad King" (1969) and "Miss Donnithorne's Maggot" (1974) are two musical compositions combining texts by

Randolph Stow with the music of Peter Maxwell Davies. The works have been performed separately, and together, most notably in April of 1974 at the Queen Elizabeth Hall, London. "Eight Songs for a Mad King" dramatizes the madness of George III. Stow writes of the piece: "One imagined the King in his purple flannel dressing gown and ermine night-cap, struggling to teach birds to make music.... Or trying to sing with them." He continues later, "The songs are to be understood as the King's monologue while listening to his birds perform, and incorporate some sentences actually spoken by George III."[3]

"Miss Donnithorne's Maggot" is a musical treatment of Miss Donnithorne of Newton, New South Wales, a jilted recluse who was possibly the model for Dickens' Miss Havisham.

The poems which form the text for both musicals are particularly suited to the modernist scores and their staging. It is difficult and perhaps not justifiable to separate Stow's words from the total production, for they are not intended to stand alone as poetry.

CHAPTER 11

Conclusion

I *Fiction*

IT is to Stow's credit, I think, that in attempting an overview of his fiction the critic is hard put to make any conventional label stick to him. He is a realist, but not in the ordinary sense of the term. He is a symbolist, an allegorist, a mythmaker, a romancer; and yet he is more than any one of these terms includes. His work shows him to be a regionalist, an Australian; and having said this, one must go on to say that the sense of the particular place is ultimately less important than the universal nature of his concerns.

The critic's job is hardly easier when he attempts a general assessment of Stow's fiction. There are the problems that make his work uneven: shifts in the level of diction, in the level of narration, and the short-cuts to characterization. And yet his talent, the poetic quality of his prose that makes reading him a pleasure, is such that the flaws in his work never seem terribly important. Let us look once again at his fiction.

Although, as we have seen, Stow is experimenting with his form in each novel and although he writes no two novels in quite the same manner, it is possible in a survey of the works to identify similar interests in all of the novels, as well as repeated problems and achievements. For the purpose of summary, let us consider the novels collectively, looking at them in terms of Stow's characters, and the themes that result from their action, at his use of setting, and finally, at his technique in general.

II *Stow's Characters*

If one were to sketch the typical protagonist who has been repeated often in Australian fiction, he would produce a figure who for the most part is robust, extrovertive, optimistic, and pragmatic.[1] Looking at any of Stow's protagonists, with the exception of the boy Rob Coram, one can see how far he departs from this traditional figure. His typical protagonist is a misfit, an outsider, an introvert, a man engaged in a search. He may be a victim of his own excessive pride and self-deception, as is Andrew Maguire in *A Haunted Land,* and as to some extent is Patrick Leighton in *The Bystander,* Heriot in *To the Islands,* and the diviner in *Tourmaline.* He may have a physical or mental deformity that separates him from others: again Andrew Maguire; and Patrick Leighton and Keithy Farnham in *The Bystander;* and Byrne in *Tourmaline.* He may have acquired his separation through brutal experiences — Diana Ravirs in *The Bystander,* Rick Maplestead in *The Merry-Go-Round in the Sea*; or through an excessive amount of self-criticism — Heriot and the diviner. For one reason or another, each of Stow's major figures stands outside conventional society; depending on his own nature, he may be either oblivious to that society; critical of it, to the point of wanting to change it; or accepting of it but unable to successfully integrate into it. He is generally, because of his sense of separateness, unhappy, lonely, restless. His restlessness takes one of several forms. He tries to hold on to the past (Andrew Maguire), to make something permanent, "something forever" (Maguire, Diana, Patrick, Keithy); he tries to insure his immortality through a metaphysical quest (Heriot, the diviner); or he decides on a walkabout in the world beyond Australia (Rick Maplestead). During the course of his attempt to deal with his isolation and his particular pain he makes several discoveries: that nothing is permanent, that houses, land, family ties, love (sexual love, metaphysical love, love of fellowman, and love of country) all fade. He discovers that pride is destructive, both to self and others (Maguire, Diana, Patrick, Heriot, Rick) and that any lack of self-reliance, any giving of one's life over to someone or something else is dangerous (all the characters to some extent, but particularly the people of Tourmaline).

From the characters' restlessness, from their attempts to deal with their isolation and loneliness, come the learning experiences and it is these experiences that form Stow's themes: stated again, the destructive nature of time and the impossibility of permanence, the destructive nature of pride and love, the danger of giving up self-reliance.

Stow's problems and his successes in characterization have been noted in the discussions of the individual novels. Working as he does with types in *A Haunted Land,* there is no significant problem, but when he moves into realistic territory in the two novels that follow, the techniques of delineation that he uses are often inadequate for the depth of characterization demanded. In *The Bystander* Stow slights Patrick Leighton, depending on a summary of Leighton's past to suggest his present condition; and in the same novel Stow resorts to cliché in an attempt to reveal the inward struggles of Diana Ravirs. The flaws in the characterizations in the novel are less serious than, but at the same time suggestive of, similar flaws that Stow repeats in *To the Islands.* As with Diana and Patrick, Stow observes Heriot too much from the outside, insisting on his motivation, his depth, his importance when he should be projecting from the inside, dramatizing, finding a correlative in action to illustrate those aspects of character on which his story rests. This problem occurs again, though to a lesser extent, with the diviner and Kestrel, and with Hugh Mackay and Jane Wexford. A further unsuccessful short-cut to characterization is Stow's use of literary quotation and allusion, an attempt at characterization by extension or association, a device Stow uses primarily in *To the Islands* with Heriot.

Stow's most successful characters are his children: Keithy in *The Bystander* and Rob in *The Merry-Go-Round in the Sea.* He seems comfortable with them, sure in his understanding of their nature and in his projection of their problems. Working in their point of view, Stow re-creates a childhood vision that rings true in its capacity for confusion, for insight, for humor, for innocence and for delight.

His least successful characters are his lovers. With the exception of Patrick and Jane in *A Haunted Land* and Michael and Deborah in *Tourmaline,* the lovers as they come together in an expression of their emotions seem awkward and stilted. While noting the ways in which Stow is outside the tradition of Australian literature, it is interesting to observe that in this one instance he takes his place in line with other Australian novelists. T. Inglis Moore in his discussion of realism points out that the treatment of love in a personal manner is seldom found in Australian literature as it is seldom found in classic American literature. When romance between two characters must be dealt with, the treatment is often bloodless or vague, as in the case of Patrick White's lovers in *Voss;* or stiff and unconvincing, as with Stow's lovers in four of the five novels.[2] Moore's accounting for this general tendency, however, does not explain Stow's difficulty. Moore describes the typical Australian writer as realistic in his outlook, dealing with an essentially masculine world, one which has little room for the theme of love, a theme, Moore says, better suited to romanticism than realism.[3] Stow's point of view in all the novels is far more poetic — i.e., romantic — than it is realistic. And thus, following Moore's reasoning, one would expect a successful treatment of romance relationships. Why Stow does falter is a question difficult to answer.

III   *Setting — The Sense of Place*

If some consistency can be found in Stow's repetition of similar characters, an even greater consistency can be found in his choice of setting and in his use of setting. As has been frequently indicated, Stow's stories unfold in and about the area of Geraldton, with the exception of *To the Islands,* which is set farther up the coast in the Kimberly Mountains of northwest Australia. Stow knows his land well, and one of the delights of reading him is in coming to an awareness of an area of such sensuous richness.

It has been said that Stow is a realist, and he is, but he is a particular kind of realist. Although the birds, the animals, the plants, the sea, the desert, the sky, the farms, and the towns are distinctly those of Western Australia, and although there is a great attention to detail in Stow, the particulars, the details, are filtered through the eyes of the poet, rendered with the faithfulness of a camera perhaps, but a camera trained on planned compositions, compositions in which the details group together to form a study. One could not walk through Geraldton and find his way around after reading Stow, nor would he find Malin or Tourmaline as Stow presents them on any local map; but all the elements that combine to create the sense of these places — the textures, the light and glare, the smells, the sand and the heat, the distinct seasons — are real in a way that a journalistic kind of realism never is. Though many examples have been given throughout this study of the poetic nature of Stow's prose, one last example will serve to illustrate how he translates realistic detail into poetic composition. Consider Stow's introduction of the character Deborah in *Tourmaline:*

> A road of daylight led from the open door to the cash-register, striking deep jewel-tones from liqueurs that will never be drunk in Tourmaline. It struck, also, a gold bangle on the wrist of Deborah, in which the sombre green of the walls merged with the tawny glimmer of her half-caste skin.
>
> It rose on Deborah herself, very tall, very straight; her back uncompromising and austere, her calm hands folded. That tallness had entered into her character, making her remote; almost, at times (that aloofness partly obscuring her) invisible. But she was timid too; the profound darkness of her eyes unwilling to be looked into. Imagine her there.[4]

Setting is important in Stow's fiction because of the poetic sense of place that he evokes through it, and further important in that it is often used as a determinant of character. It is not so much that a character is inescapably molded by his immediate environment, made victim by it in the sense that philosophical naturalism would have it, as it is that a character is strongly conditioned by his surroundings. Malin is to *A Haunted Land* what Wuthering Heights is to that novel. Heriot's personality, his sense of spiritual isolation and loneliness, is heightened through his long years of geographical isolation at the mission. The people of Tourmaline, cut off from the rest of the world by their desert isolation, interact in a way that a people with the possibility of communication beyond the limits of their town would not. As an influence on character, one might add that setting is also important to Stow's work because of his own interest in the particular Australian nature of his places. While his concerns are universal enough that any isolated place might serve as the setting for *A Haunted Land, The Bystander,* or *Tourmaline,* and any small town and its environs might serve as a background to play out his insights into childhood, his interest in communicating a sense of what is specifically regional, uniquely Australian is what, given his descriptive powers, makes his fiction outstanding.

IV   *Technique*

In each of his five novels Stow is experimenting, to one degree or another, with technique, employing various devices to structure his material, to reveal character, and to express and expand his themes.

Geoffrey Dutton has placed Stow's work in "the tradition of the novel as dramatic poetry."[5] Certainly Stow makes use of dramatic structuring, particularly in his first two novels. The unfolding of the story in *A Haunted Land* depends on the entrance and exits of the characters, and in *The Bystander* the structure is composed of a succession of individual scenes, each clearly distinct. Though the dramatic method is less obvious in *To the Islands* and *Tourmaline,* Stow returns to it in *The Merry-Go-Round in the Sea*, fading his scenes in and out with a continuation of thought from one to the other that serves a purpose similar to the dimming, darkening, and relighting of the stage as scenic transitions are called for.

In the novels other than *To the Islands* and *Tourmaline,* Stow makes use of weather and seasonal change as a structural device, often paralleling a character's state of mind, or a climactic change in the novel, with a change in weather or season. This is particularly the case in the first two novels; and in *The Merry-Go-Round in the Sea* Stow indicates both passage of time and character development in terms of seasonal change, structuring often around a cataloguing of one sense impression, sound or smell, as Rob Coram learns the difference between times of the year and between the town and the country.

Looking at Stow's general approach, Geoffrey Dutton writes:

> Stow always sees literature as extended metaphor, connecting human life to something else, usually to land, sometimes a house (Malin, Lingarin, Koolabye), birds, or animals, a town (Tourmaline). In this sense all his writing is poetic. Even when he is writing most realistically he is apt to extend his references.[6]

The extension of reference is found in each of Stow's novels. As the Maguire family falls apart, so does Malin. The characters in *A Haunted Land* are isolated spiritually from one another even as their farms stand alone; the cry of the plover echoes Keithy's despair, and as he runs into the burning woods the screeching cockatoos share his frenzy as they seem to shout his name. Diana sees herself through Keithy's eyes in terms of a snake, as Keithy tells her that he dislikes snakes because "snakes can never love anyone." The beauty of a young crocodile, a wallaby, geese in flight suggest God to Heriot, and his physical journey through the outback is a metaphor for the spiritual journey he is undertaking.

Tourmaline is a microcosm of a world in hope of spiritual regeneration, and the crow that cries above it sounds the loneliness of man
lost in space. Rob Coram's romantic merry-go-round in the sea is
Rick Maplestead's "big world" beyond Australia.

Stow's tendency to see things in terms of correspondence led
him, no doubt, easily from a limited use of metaphor to the extensive use he makes of it in *To the Islands* and in *Tourmaline*. While
he is successful with metaphor throughout the novels on a limited
scale, he gets into trouble as he expands into conceits, into the allegorical. The problems in character delineation in *To the Islands* and
in correspondence in *Tourmaline* have been noted and explained.
Stow's problems in the projection of character into symbol, in the
case of Heriot and to a lesser extent with the diviner, suggest an
irony. His poetic approach, the aspect of his work that makes it
outstanding, is at the same time in part responsible for the flaws in
the novel. Vincent Buckley's assessment of Heriot, that "he is far
too vague to bear the mythopoetic weight Stow puts on him,"[7]
illustrates this problem. While vagueness is often a desirable effect
of a symbol within a poem, an effect the poet often works for, symbolic vagueness as an aspect of characterization, especially when
the meaning of the novel is dependent on the clear delineation of
character, is a detriment. As a poet, Stow senses the limitations of
realism and in his fiction he attempts to overcome these limitations,
at the same time remaining unwilling to abandon realism altogether. In his effort he is not altogether successful, although he
comes much closer to success in *The Merry-Go-Round in the Sea*
than in the two novels that precede it. In the latter novel the poetic
use of image and metaphor is retained, while the heavy dependence
on symbol and myth is discarded.

V   Summary of Poetry

As does his fiction, Randolph Stow's poetry also resists an easy
label. His poetry shows him to be well acquainted with traditional
Western literature, and he uses its myths, its subjects, its conventions, and its forms to his own purposes. At the same time he is an
Australian, and his poetic interests are often those expressed by his
predecessors and contemporaries. He, as so many Australian poets,
is deeply affected by the land, and his poetry reflects a number of
identifiable Australian poetic characteristics: somberness, realism,

irony, and satire. He is a nature poet, but just as he records its beauty, he also records its danger.

Stow concerns himself with typical Australian subjects: the sea coast, the homestead, the outback, exploration, loneliness, mateship, alienation, and expatriation. Just as he manipulates English poetic conventions, he uses for his own purposes the Australian bush ballad and the "voyager poems" of exploration. He looks at his subjects in a variety of ways: through the eyes of children, through mythological and historical figures, through both personal and impersonal narrators. Although a few of his poems in *Outrider* are mental, hazy, confessional, as is common with a certain strain of the poetry of the 1950s and 1960s, his poetry is generally free, as is much of Australian poetry, from rhetoric and esoteric intellectualism. His poetry is for the most part traditional and not experimental.

In style, Stow's best poetry is characterized by a certain crispness. His images are clear, his diction precise and economical. Although his poems may on occasion be long — one is 232 lines — they are usually short; and although his stanzas sometimes are composed of as many as ten lines, he works often with the ballad stanza and with the epigrammatic one and two line stanza, which is well suited for the directness of his observations.

While Stow is a realist, in a number of his poems, particularly those with non-Australian subjects, there is a romantic Keatsian, Pre-Raphaelite quality in his use of sensual images. Often his realistic poems, even those about unhappy subjects — disease, destruction — are through a selection of images made romantic and appealing.

Critical assessment of Stow's poetry has ranged from the strong praise for *Act One* to a lessening of enthusiasm for *Outrider* and the new poems in *A Counterfeit Silence*. Critics point to a slackness, a searching after direction in certain poems in these volumes, while singling out for positive attention certain stanzas and lines.

VI *Last Thoughts*

Randolph Stow began to write in Australia at a very early age, publishing the largest portion of his writing before he was thirty. That writing, for the most part the content of this study, is describable in terms of Stow's youthful experiences — geographical, psychological, practical, and literary.

Of the last sixteen years or so, Randolph Stow has lived only three years in Australia, traveling some, but living much of the time near London. The experiences of his thirties do not duplicate those of his twenties, nor doubtlessly will the literature that incorporates these experiences. In the past few years he has continued to publish criticism and an occasional poem and has ventured into music as a librettist. He also continues to write fiction, withholding to date for his own reasons that fiction from publication.

To attempt to assess the career of a working writer just now into his forties would be presumptuous. Randolph Stow is, as his work illustrates, a man of tenderness, talent, and vision. With a great appreciation for the works described in this volume, I eagerly anticipate those works still to come.

Notes and References

Chapter One

1. Geoffrey Dutton, "The Search for Permanence in the Novels of Randolph Stow," *Journal of Commonwealth Literature,* 1 (1965), 135–48.
2. John Hetherington, "Young Man in No Hurry," *Forty-two Faces,* (Melbourne, 1962), p. 244.
3. Ibid., p. 245.
4. Granville Hicks, review of *To the Islands,* by Randolph Stow, *Saturday Review,* 12 September 1959, p. 22.
5. Randolph Stow, jacket of *The Merry-Go-Round in the Sea,* (New York, 1966).
6. T. Inglis Moore, *Social Patterns in Australian Literature,* (Berkeley, 1971), pp. 13–15.
7. Ibid., pp. 12–21.
8. Hetherington, p. 242.

Chapter Two

1. Randolph Stow, *A Haunted Land* (London, 1956), p. 39. All further citations refer to this edition and are indicated by page numbers placed at the end of the reference.
2. P.H. Newby, "The Novels of Randolph Stow," *Australian Letters,* I (November 1957), 49–52.
3. Ibid.
4. Vincent Buckley, "In the Shadow of Patrick White," *Meanjin,* XX, 2 (1961), 144–54.
5. David Martin, "Among the Bones," *Meanjin,* XVIII, 1 (1957), 52–58.
6. Dutton, p. 143.
7. Nathaniel Hawthorne, *The Scarlet Letter* (New York, 1961), p. 31.
8. Leonie Kramer, "The Novels of Randolph Stow," *Southerly,* XXIV, 2 (1964), 84.
9. Ibid.
10. Ibid.
11. Ibid., p. 89.

12. Dutton, p. 141.

13. Kramer, pp. 80–81.

14. Dutton, p. 140.

15. Hetherington, p. 246.

16. G.W.K. Johnston, "The Art of Randolph Stow," *Meanjin,* XX, (1961), 143.

17. Dutton, p. 139.

18. Ibid.

Chapter Three

1. Randolph Stow, *The Bystander* (London, 1957), p. 9. All further citations refer to this edition and are indicated by page numbers placed at the end of the reference.

2. Dutton, p. 141.

3. Newby, p. 50.

4. Kramer, p. 86.

5. Ibid.

6. Newby, p. 50.

7. Dutton, p. 141.

Chapter Four

1. Hicks, p. 12.

2. Kramer, p. 80.

3. Randolph Stow, *To the Islands* (London, 1958), pp. 11-12. All further citations refer to this edition and are indicated by page numbers placed at the end of the reference.

4. Review of *To the Islands,* by Randolph Stow, *Times Literary Supplement,* 2 January 1959, p. 5.

5. Kramer, p. 79.

6. Martin, p. 52.

7. G.K. Johnston, review of *To the Islands,* by Randolph Stow, *Quadrant,* III, 4 (1959), 87-89.

8. Kramer, p. 79.

9. Buckley, p. 148.

10. Ibid.

11. Dutton, p. 44.

12. Moore, p. 90.

13. Buckley, p. 148.

Chapter Five

1. Randolph Stow, *Tourmaline* (Melbourne, 1965), p. 7. All further citations refer to this edition and are indicated by page numbers placed at the end of the reference.

2. Kramer, p. 88.

3. Ibid.

4. A.D. Hope, "Randolph Stow and the Tourmaline Affair," in *The Australian Experience,* ed. W.S. Ransom (Canberra, 1974), p. 264.

Chapter Six

1. Randolph Stow, *The Merry-Go-Round in the Sea* (London, 1965). pp. 34–35, 36. All further citations refer to this edition and are indicated by page numbers placed at the end of the reference.

2. Neil McPherson, "Writers for a 'No' Generation," *Westerly,* I (August 1966), 61.

3. Ibid.

4. Maurice Shadbolt, "The Flight from Innocence," *Bulletin,* LXXXVII (25 December 1965), 35–36.

Chapter Seven

1. Randolph Stow, *Act One* (London, 1957), pp. 15–18. All further citations are taken from this text.

Chapter Eight

1. Randolph Stow, *Outrider* (London, 1962), p. 11. All further citations are taken from this text.

Chapter Nine

1. Thornton Wilder, *The Bridge of San Luis Rey* (U.S.A., 1927), p. 97.

2. Randolph Stow, *A Counterfeit Silence* (Sydney, 1969), p. 51. All poetry quotations in this chapter are taken from this text.

3. James Legge, trans., *The Texts of Taoism* (New York, 1959), p. 98.

Chapter Ten

1. Randolph Stow, "Dokónikan," in *Australian Writing Today,* ed. Charles Higham (Harmondsworth, Middlesex, 1968), p. 296.

2. Randolph Stow, "Dokónikan," p. 288.

3. Randolph Stow, "Eight Songs for a Mad King," *The Fires of London Program* (London, 23 April, 1974).

Chapter Eleven

1. Dutton, p. 147.
2. Moore, pp. 118–22.
3. Ibid., p. 118.
4. Stow, *Tourmaline*, pp. 10–11.
5. Dutton, p. 143.
6. Ibid., p. 146.
7. Buckley, p. 148.

Selected Bibliography

PRIMARY SOURCES

In this section I have listed only the English language editions of Stow's most important works. Translations are noted in the chronology. I have not listed uncollected poems, essays, or reviews. For these works, I refer the reader to one of the bibliographies mentioned in the following section of secondary sources.

I   Poetry

Act One: Poems. London: Macdonald, 1957.
Outrider: Poems, 1956–62, with paintings by Sidney Nolan. London: Macdonald, 1957.
Poems from "The Outrider" and Other Poems, illustrated by Sidney Nolan. Adelaide: Australian Letters, 1963. (Australian artists and poets booklet no. 9)
A Counterfeit Silence: Selected Poems. Sydney: Angus & Robertson, 1969.
Randolph Stow Reads from His Own Work. St. Lucia, Queensland: University of Queensland Press, 1974. (Poets on Record Series, No. 11)

II   Novels and Other Fiction

A Haunted Land. London: Macdonald, 1956. New York: Macmillan, 1957.
The Bystander. London: Macdonald, 1957.
To the Islands. London: Macdonald, 1958. Boston: Little, Brown, 1959. Melbourne: Penguin Books, 1962.
Tourmaline. London: Macdonald, 1963. Melbourne: Penguin Books, 1965.
The Merry-Go-Round in the Sea. London: Macdonald, 1965. New York, Morrow, 1966. Melbourne: Penguin Books, 1968.
Midnite: The Story of a Wild Colonial Boy. Melbourne: Cheshire, 1967. Englewood Cliffs, N.J.: Prentice-Hall, 1968. London: Puffin Books, 1969. A children's book and a satire.
"Magic," a short story, in *Modern Australian Writing,* ed. Geoffrey Dutton, pp. 106–19. London: Fontana, 1966.

"Dokónikan," a short story, in *Australian Writing Today,* ed. Charles Higham, pp. 287–96. Harmondsworth, Middlesex: Penguin, 1968.

III   Editorial Work

Australian Poetry, 1964, edited by Randolph Stow. Sydney: Angus & Robertson, 1964.

IV   Texts to Musical Compositions

Eight Songs for a Mad King, music by Peter Maxwell Davies. London: Boosey and Hawkes, 1971; recording: Unicorn RHS 308, 1972.
Miss Donnithorne's Maggot, music by Peter Maxwell Davies. Text in *The Fires of London Program.* London: 23 April 1974.

SECONDARY SOURCES

I   Useful Bibliographical Guides

"Annual Bibliography of Studies in Australian Literature" in *Australian Literary Studies.* May issue of each year.
BESTON, ROSE MARIE. "Principles of Selection of Bibliographical Items." *The Literary Half-yearly,* XVI, 2 (1975), 137–44. This is a publication of The Center for Commonwealth Literature and Research, University of Mysore, India. The July 1975 issue contains a useful biographical essay and this bibliography, of particular value because it updates the Stow material through 1974.
O'BRIEN, PATRICIA. *Randolph Stow: A Bibliography.* Adelaide: Libraries Board of South Australia, 1968. This is the most comprehensive bibliography on Stow, and an excellent one.

II   Useful Sources of Biographical Information

BESTON, JOHN B. "The Family Background and Literary Career of Randolph Stow." *The Literary Half-yearly,* XVI, 2 (1975), 125–33.
DUTTON, GEOFFREY. "The Search for Permanence in the Novels of Randolph Stow." *Journal of Commonwealth Literature,* 1 (1965), 135–48.
HETHERINGTON, JOHN. "Young Man in No Hurry." *Forty-two Faces,* pp. 242–47. Melbourne: Cheshire, 1962.

III   Criticism

The following bibliography is divided into two lists. In the first I cite works which I have used directly or indirectly in the writing of this book. The essays are annotated. The reviews are not, but are useful to the student for a comment or a phrase which provides insight into the individual work. In the second list I have cited works which I have not used, in some cases have not read. I offer these as a further sampling of the critical material available. For a more complete or a more up-to-date bibliography, I refer the reader to the guides noted in Part I.

Works Consulted

ALLSOP, KENNETH. "Delicate Wiring." *Spectator,* 31 December 1969, p. 869. Essay on *The Merry-Go-Round in the Sea.* Discusses point of view.

AUCHTERLONE, D. Review of *Outrider,* by Randolph Stow. *Quadrant,* VIII (Autumn 1963), 91–95.

BUCKLEY, VINCENT. "In the Shadow of Patrick White." *Meanjin,* XX, 2 (1961), 144–54. Good discussion of *To the Islands;* deals with problems in Heriot's characterization.

"Christ or Lucifer." Review of *Tourmaline,* by Randolph Stow. *Times Literary Supplement,* 5 April 1963, p. 229.

CURLE, J. J. "Randolph Stow: Poet and Novelist." *Poetry Review,* XLIX (January-March 1958), 9–17. Sensitive, appreciative discussion of Stow's work by the Macdonald's editor who has worked with Stow throughout most of his publishing career.

DUTTON, GEOFFREY. "The Search for Permanence in the Novels of Randolph Stow." *Journal of Commonwealth Literature,* 1 (1965), 135–48. A good, useful basic essay on Stow. Discusses structure and theme in first four novels. Brief biographical sketch.

EPSY, J. J. Review of *To the Islands,* by Randolph Stow. *New York Herald Tribune Book Review,* 18 October 1957, p. 12.

GREEN, HENRY M. *A History of Australian Literature,* 2 vols. Sydney: Angus and Robertson, 1961. Background information; places Stow in the development of Australian literature.

HEMMINGS, F. W. J. Review of *The Merry-Go-Round in the Sea,* by Randolph Stow. *New Statesman,* LXX (22 October 1965), 613.

HETHERINGTON, JOHN. "Young Man in No Hurry." *Forty-two Faces,* pp. 242–47. Melbourne: Cheshire, 1962. Good biographical source; some insight into the fiction.

HICKS, GRANVILLE. Review of *Tourmaline,* by Randolph Stow. *Saturday Review,* 12 September 1969, p. 22.

HOPE, A. D. "Randolph Stow and the Tourmaline Affair." In *The Australian Experience,* ed. W. S. Ramson, pp. 249–68. Canberra: Australian National University Press, 1974.

HUTCHINSON, DAVID. Review of *Tourmaline,* by Randolph Stow. *Westerly,* 3 (1963), 77–80.

JOHNSTON, G. K. W. "The Art of Randolph Stow." *Meanjin,* XX, 2 (1961), 139–43. Study of the first three novels. Faults Stow for Tommy Cross as structural device in *A Haunted Land* and for characters in *To the Islands.*

_____ . Review of *To the Islands,* by Randolph Stow, *Quadrant,* III, 4 (1959), 87–89.

JONES, JOSEPH AND JOHANNA. *Authors and Areas of Australia.* Austin: Steck-Vaughn, 1970. Picture, brief description of Stow's works.

KRAMER, LEONIE. "Heritage of Dust." *Bulletin,* XXCIV (6 July 1963), 41. Brief discussion of *Tourmaline.*

_____ . "Stow's Riotous Garden." *Bulletin,* LXXXVIII (8 December 1962), 38. Brief discussion of *Outrider.*

_____ . "The Novels of Randolph Stow." *Southerly,* XXIV, 2 (1964), 78–91. Lengthy, good, useful essay on Stow's first four novels, though I don't always agree with Kramer's observations.

LEE, S. E. "Confessional and Experimental Verse." *Southerly,* XXX, 4 (1970), 306–308. A useful discussion of the new poems in *A Counterfeit Silence.*

LEGGE, JAMES, trans. *The Texts of Taoism.* New York: The Julian Press, 1959.

LEWIS, J. "Broad and Bitter." Review of *Tourmaline,* by Randolph Stow. *Spectator,* 5 April 1963, p. 440.

MANSTEN, S. P. Review of *A Haunted Land,* by Randolph Stow, *Saturday Review,* 11 May 1957, p. 15.

MARTIN, DAVID. "Among the Bones." *Meanjin,* XVIII, 1 (1959), 52–58. Good essay on first three novels. Offers a definition of the kind of poetic novel Stow writes. Good discussion of Heriot in *To the Islands.*

_____ . Review of *A Haunted Land,* by Randolph Stow. *Meanjin,* XVI, 1 (1957), 88–89.

MCPHERSON, NEIL. "Writers for a 'No' Generation." *Westerly,* I (1966), 59–62. Useful criticism of *The Merry-Go-Round in the Sea.* Discusses the merry-go-round as a symbol.

MOORE, T. INGLIS. *Social Patterns in Australian Literature.* Berkeley: University of California Press, 1971. Excellent study. Not a great deal on Stow, but good for indicating the literary foreground, with some discussion of contemporary literature.

NEWBY, P. H. "The Novels of Randolph Stow." *Australian Letters,* I (November 1957), 49–51. A discussion of *A Haunted Land* and *The Bystander,* style and characters.

O'BRIEN, PATRICIA. *Randolph Stow: A Bibliography.* Adelaide: South Australia Libraries Board, 1968. The most extensive bibliography.

PHILLIPS, ARTHUR A. Review of *To the Islands,* by Randolph Stow. *Overland,* 15 (1959), 51–52.

"Poet and Painter." Review of *Outrider,* by Randolph Stow. *Times Literary Supplement,* 28 June 1963, p. 472.

"Rob's Rick." Review of *The Merry-go-round in the Sea,* by Randolph Stow. *Times Literary Supplement,* 18 November 1965, p. 1028.

ROSENTHAL, T. G. Review of *Outrider,* by Randolph Stow. *Australian Book Review,* II (January 1963), 43.

SHADBOLT, MAURICE. "The Flight From Innocence." *Bulletin* LXXXVII (25 December 1965), 35-36. Favorable impression of *The Merry-Go-Round in the Sea.*

TAUBMAN, R. Review of *Tourmaline,* by Randolph Stow. *New Statesman,* LXV (24 May 1963), 802.

"The First Act." *Southerly,* XIX, 2 (1958), 105-106. Good, although brief discussion of *Act One.*

WILDER, THORNTON. *The Bridge of San Luis Rey.* U.S.A: Grosset and Dunlap, 1927.

Selected Additional Bibliography

BURGESS, O. N. "The Novels of Randolph Stow." *Australian Quarterly,* XXXVII, 1 (1965), 73-81.

GEERING, R. G. *Recent Fiction.* Australian Writers and Their Work Series. Pp. 1-30. Melbourne: Oxford University Press, 1973.

HASSALL, ANTHONY J. "Full Circle: Randolph Stow's *The Merry-Go-Round in the Sea.*" *Meanjin,* XXXII, 1 (1973), 58-64.

HOPE, A. D. "Randolph Stow and the Way to Heaven." *Hemisphere,* XVIII, 6 (June 1974), 33-35.

MARTIN, PHILIP. "Randolph Stow as Poet." *Twentieth Century* (Aust.), XII (Winter 1958), 349-52.

NEW, WILLIAM. "Outsider Looking Out: The Novels of Randolph Stow." *Critique: Studies in Modern Fiction,* IX, 1 (1967), 90-99.

OPPEN, ALICE. "Myth and Reality in Randolph Stow." *Southerly,* XXVII, 2 (1967), 82-94.

WHITEHEAD, JEAN. "The Individualism of Randolph Stow." In *Sandgropers: A Western Australian Anthology,* ed. Dorothy Hewett, pp. 181-87. Nedlands: University of Western Australia Press, 1973.

WIGHTMAN, JENNIFER. "Waste Places, Dry Souls: The Novels of Randolph Stow." *Meanjin,* XXVIII (June 1969), 239-52.

Index

156